In the Shadows

In the shadows

DAVID STOCKS

work
for good.

Matador
Unit E2 Airfield Business Park
Harrison Road, Market Harborough
Leicestershire LE16 7UL
Tel: 0116 279 2299
Email: books@troubador.co.uk
Web: www.troubador.co.uk/matador
Twitter: @matadorbooks

ISBN 978 1 80313 727 8

British Library Cataloguing in Publication Data.
A catalogue record for this book is available from the British Library.

Printed and bound by CPI Group (UK) Ltd, Croydon, CR0 4YY
Typeset in 11pt Minion Pro by Troubador Publishing Ltd, Leicester, UK

Matador is an imprint of Troubador Publishing Ltd

MIX
Paper | Supporting
responsible forestry
FSC
www.fsc.org   FSC® C013604

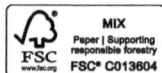

'To Mum and Dad, who supported me during the early days of my football career. Also to my wonderful wife, Debs, and my three boys, Ollie, Alex and Marc.'

CONTENTS

In The Shadows

ACKNOWLEDGEMENTS

I would like to thank everyone who has helped in any way with this book, especially the following:

Neil Vacher from AFC Bournemouth for providing me with photographs from my playing days and giving valuable advice during the book's production.

Tom Crocker from the *Bournemouth Daily Echo* for his assistance with my enquiries.

Terry Gulliver, Ted MacDougall, Keith Peacock, Dave Thomas and Steve Webb for their valuable contributions and recollections. They have helped to shine a light down memory lane.

Katherine Stracey and Jack Wright for proofreading the manuscript.

Briony Duguid for designing the cover.

Ben Hayes and Paul Baker from the Charlton Athletic

Museum for their incredible help in furnishing me with stats and photos from my time there.

Richard Hughes from the *Herald Express* for furnishing me with information on my time at Torquay.

Dominic Mee from Torquay United for providing me with detailed fixture and line-up information.

Allan Tyrer from gillinghamfcscrapbook.co.uk for hosting information on my time at Gillingham.

Steve Wright for kindly helping to uncover memories long forgotten with his skilled questioning and editing.

And finally my lovely wife Debra, who has patiently typed up my rambling notes and managed to organise the numerous photos and newspaper cuttings that my parents had painstakingly and lovingly kept of my football career.

INTRODUCTION

I have been lucky enough to experience two very fulfilling careers in two very different fields. However, it was only during the second of these – my occupation as a financial consultant – that my first career as a professional footballer triggered questions and conversations. This interest came as a surprise to me. In my eyes, my 16-year spell as a professional footballer was not worthy of much conversation. Regardless, as various business connections and clients started to find out about my past, the stories and memories came flooding out.

It was during some of those long, alcohol-soaked lunches that I would be pressed by my football-obsessed business associates and clients to divulge the secrets of their heroes. They would sit in awe at my anecdotes and tales of footballing heroes such as Sir Stanley Matthews, Emlyn Hughes, Sir Geoff Hurst and the like. Having represented their country at the highest level, they would then have to face a young, enthusiastic defender on the muddy turf of The Valley.

I've had the fortune – or in some cases, misfortune – to play at some of the country's top stadiums, such as Anfield, Stamford Bridge, Maine Road, Upton Park and Elland Road, to name a few. Most importantly, there were the four I was able to call home at one point or another: The Valley for Charlton, Priestfield for Gillingham, Dean Court for Bournemouth and, finally, Plainmoor for Torquay.

On a number of occasions, I was told that I should write a book regaling my experiences, as they were deemed to be fascinating insights into the world behind the scenes of professional football. However, I resisted these entreaties for a while, as to me, they were just tales of a young lad playing in the shadows of the greats. I never felt that my stories would be of particular interest to most people, but time has passed, and now my children, family and friends are keen to hear about this time in my life. I realised that if I didn't write them down, they would be lost forever. I appreciate that they aren't going to be tabloid exposé material, but they are a part of my – and by extension, football's – history. Thus, I became motivated to dig out newspaper cuttings, programmes and various documents I had kept in the cupboard over the years.

It has taken until my retirement years, and, being in my seventies and with time on my hands, I have finally succumbed to the pressures and demands to put pen to paper. Here it goes – I do hope you enjoy it…

David Stocks

ONE

THE BEGINNING –
SCHOOLBOY AND EARLY DAYS

It all started on the streets of a post-Second World War south London – Dulwich, to be precise. Born in 1943, as a child I had no real understanding of the tumultuous events that were rumbling along in the background. The war and the immediate tell-tales of its legacy, such as the assorted bomb sites that seemed to be scattered everywhere, the implementation of food rationing, and the various rebuilding projects undertaken in the local neighbourhoods, seemed to me unremarkable facts of life. I had never known anything different, so why would they be unusual?

At the time, Dulwich was arguably one of the more upmarket areas of the capital. Having originally lived in West Norwood, my family had been relocated there into a temporary prefab property following the demolition of our house courtesy of one of Adolf Hitler's bomb attacks. Fortunately, we were not in the house at the time, being safely homed in a nearby bomb shelter. For us, this was the local church, conveniently located just across the road from where we lived. Most bomb shelters generally took the form of tube stations, but we weren't close enough to one (the nearest was about an hour away by bus, and I don't think Hitler would have been sufficiently gracious to wait long enough for us to get there before releasing the bombs).

While I was too young to remember the war itself, it cast a shadow over much of my childhood. As well as the obvious physical effects of the aforementioned destruction, food rationing remained in place until 1954. However, thanks to the attributes of our new home, we were well placed to cope. One of the biggest advantages of our new residence was a sizeable back garden, in which we were encouraged to grow our own fruit and vegetables in order to supplement the rationed food. We also kept chickens, which, as well as providing us with a steady supply of eggs, played their part in contributing to a great feast on the occasion when my grandad would select one for the oven. For a youngster, it all seemed a bit barbaric – watching him chase the poor bird around the back garden before catching and strangling it! He would then pluck and prepare it as part of the festivities for a special family occasion, such as Christmas or a birthday.

My grandparents lived in a terraced house halfway between my home and first school, West Norwood Primary, which we walked to each day. Later on, I was given a bike, but wasn't allowed to take it to school, so I would drop it off at my grandparents' house and walk the rest of the way. It was only when I started at secondary school that I was allowed to ride directly there, as there was a shed where we could chain up and store our bikes.

There weren't many bikes available to buy in the years after the war, but somehow my mum and dad managed to find the money to purchase one for me. It was a great way of getting around, especially as there was very little traffic on the roads. When I was a bit older – maybe fifteen or sixteen years of age – a group of us would sometimes cycle down to Brighton and back in a day. It was a round trip of around 100 miles – quite an achievement back then, and would obviously take up the whole day. Once there, we would sit on the beach, eat our sandwiches, jump on our bikes and ride back home! Just imagine doing that nowadays with all the traffic. You would probably be unsurprised to hear that back then in the late 1950s, the roads were a lot less busy and a great deal safer.

Despite the circumstances, post-war London was still a fun place to grow up in. Even so, life could be hard in a number of respects: many people had lost everything, the rebuilding process was lengthy, and a lot of items remained in short supply.

Our playtime in the capital was spent on the streets among the bomb sites and general carnage that lingered following the war. Unexploded devices remained a hazard, with one of our pastimes consisting of spotting and subsequently reporting them to the police or any nearby adult. It may seem like a scary thought now, but to us it was

3

all fun and games – the thought that we were potentially close to a fiery and explosive demise never crossed our minds! This aside, our salvation from boredom came in the form of anything that was round and/or bore sufficient resemblance to a ball that could be used to play games such as football or cricket. For the latter, a lamppost that had survived the Luftwaffe would suffice for the wicket, and a piece of wood salvaged from a bomb site made do for the bat.

As you would probably expect considering the subject matter of this book and my subsequent direction in life, the most popular game among myself and my friends was football. With the relative lack of road traffic in those days, the streets would serve as the pitch, with the goalposts comprising either more debris or somebody's jumper or coat. Full-scale matches would take place with two or three aside, including an 'ish' (today I believe the term is 'rush') goalkeeper. On the odd occasion there would be up to ten players on each side, the reinforcements being children from neighbouring areas. An actual football was a luxury – most matches were played with whatever there was to hand, which was often a tennis ball. It may not meet basic regulations now, but its size was quite useful, as it could be put in your pocket and taken to the school playground so the game could continue at break times or after school.

To give our games additional excitement and meaning, the playground would be given a temporary moniker: 'Highbury', 'Stamford Bridge' 'White Hart Lane' or some other London-based amphitheatre were popular choices.

These would take place while the other, non-football-playing pupils were in the playground at the same time, providing us with excellent opportunities to sharpen our ball skills as we attempted to navigate around these inadvertent pitch invaders. There was no need for football shirts (not that we would have been able to afford to buy them, in any case!); we simply passed to our mates. None of us had trainers either – the games were played in school shoes, which occasionally created problems on the home front. My mum would get suspicious as to my activities, what with my shoes being badly scuffed and bearing the tendency to wear out far more quickly than they usually would.

At this stage I didn't really support any clubs or have any favourite players, mainly because I didn't get the chance to watch enough games to form a preference. Getting to any matches was very difficult: the closest league club to me was Crystal Palace – at least an hour away by bus. There wasn't anything like the level of TV coverage in those days, too: for much of my youth, the only games to get televised were FA Cup finals and the occasional international, so pretty much all we learned about football was either from newspapers or via word of mouth. However, as I got older and started to travel with my friends, we went to watch Fulham and occasionally Chelsea and Arsenal.

After this, I would say that Fulham was the first team I supported. They were in the First Division, with outstanding players like Johnny Haynes – in my opinion the best midfielder in the country at the time – and future World Cup winner George Cohen. However, I was most interested in watching their left-back, Jim Langley. This was the position I was increasingly finding myself playing in, and it was his style that I based my own on. It was a fairly new approach for the time: for a full-back to attack as well as defend, breaking forward to supplement the attacking players.

-

During my latter years at West Norwood Secondary Modern School, it became clear that my football and cricketing talents were at a higher level than that of most of my school chums. However, my parents were determined to not let me put all my eggs in one basket and insisted that I focus on my schoolwork. This was not an unreasonable request, as although I enjoyed my sporting activities, I didn't harbour any real dreams or aspirations of becoming a professional sportsman at that point. This was a time when a career in professional sport was not viewed as anything special, especially in football. This all changed after England won the World Cup in 1966. The increased amount of television coverage, catalysed by the debut of the BBC's Match of the Day in 1964, started to open up a wider audience to the game.

Formal education had, understandably, taken a back seat for the majority of the population during the war, and there was a real drive to generate a well-educated and hard-working work force to help get the country back on track. There was a good balance between academic study and sport at my school. It was rightly felt that team spirit was an important factor in fostering the kind of skills that would come to be of importance in later life. This is a belief that I still possess today.

In the late 1950s and early 1960s, football clubs did not have the same structure and elaborate scouting networks as they do nowadays, not to mention the level of financial support that now exists at the top level. At this point, no one was being recruited to top-flight academies at eight years of age (or in some cases, even younger!) as they are now. In my case, the first instance of having my potential to play at a higher level recognised occurred when I was selected for both South London Schools' cricket and football teams.

Like football, cricket in those days bore no resemblance to its setup today. There were certainly no one-day or 20/20 matches; just three-day county matches and five-day test matches at international level, mainly against the likes of the West Indies, Australia and India. Having played for South London, this opened up the possibility of selection for Surrey & London, which was the next representative stepping stone. It was also rumoured that I was very close to being picked for the England cricket team at schoolboy level, partly due to the fact that my combination of right-hand bat and left-hand fast bowling was unusual. There weren't many who could claim to be a competent batter *and* left-arm swing bowler, so in that regard I stood out. Like pretty much every other sport around this time, cricket was not financially backed at the same level as it is now. Payment for playing professionally was very low, although careers tended to last longer than they did in football. Players could very easily carry on into their late thirties and forties, and, on the odd occasion, their fifties.

I think my love of sport, especially football and cricket, was probably inherited from my father. Before the war, he had enjoyed playing football and cricket in local teams. He served in the tank regiment in France, but never really spoke about his experiences – like most, he was a very brave man. Sadly, he lost a leg after his tank was hit by a German shell, which put paid to most of his sporting activities. While this obviously meant that he couldn't play football again, a combination of determination, derring-do and ingenuity that is often brought out in the most challenging of situations meant he was still able to play cricket for a local team. He couldn't bowl, but was able to continue batting, with a teammate on hand to complete his runs for him. Fielding was conveniently done in the slips.

This kind of arrangement was far from unusual in those days, as a considerable number of men returned from the war with significant injuries. Their local teams welcomed them, finding ways for them to keep on participating. The war left a lasting impact on everyone's lives, but there was a great sense of camaraderie within the sporting world. This brought with it a determination to show support for the brave men who had returned from the war, whether their ailments were physical or mental. It was this kind of spirit that helped the country gradually return to a sense of normality after so many difficult years. On reflection, despite being borne out of the most tragic of circumstances, these were incredible times.

Back then, county cricket teams consisted of both full-time professionals and amateurs, as counties could not afford to fund full professional sides. The amateurs tended to be made up of the cream of the local cricket clubs, so anyone from a postman to a local solicitor could represent their county if they were good enough. If I were growing up today, I think it's likely that I would have been more tempted towards a career in cricket, which is far better financially supported as a career now, especially with the massively increased level of television coverage.

One phenomenon in those days was the existence of a number of individuals who not only played cricket professionally, but also did the same for football. Notable among this number were the likes of Dennis and Leslie Compton, who played for Arsenal and Middlesex, and a number of players at Charlton Athletic, such as Derek Upton, Stuart Leary and Fred Lucas, who played for Kent during the '50s and '60s. Football normally took precedence for these sporting all-rounders, who would play the full football season before moving over to cricket for the summer months. They would then report back to their football clubs around the end of July and early August in preparation for pre-season training. It was an incredible arrangement, and one that would not have been conceivable in today's professional game. This was especially the case with there being so little time between the end of one season and the beginning of the next, even if you take international tournaments into account. Most players seem to prefer to jet off to somewhere hot and sunny during their downtime, which I can't really blame them for! Even so, with people who are good at one sport tending to also be adept at another, this sporting double-life continued to be the case for many individuals for quite a while. As recently as 1978-85, Ian Botham was combining playing cricket for Somerset and England with occasional appearances for Yeovil Town and Scunthorpe United.

As it was, while I approached the end of my time at school, I became keen to use my football talent for a career path. Around this time, I progressed to playing for London Schoolboys, which saw us face off against the likes of Manchester, Birmingham and Berlin. My teammates included a number of future professionals: Terry Venables, Les Picking, Roger Hugo, Eddie Presland, Mike Broad and Allan Harris (brother of Ron 'Chopper' Harris of Chelsea fame) were among their number. As you would probably expect, Venables stood out. He was the best player I played with and against. When you were on his side, the tactics were simple: you gave him the ball. He was as good at the age of 15 as he was at the peak of his career, which isn't intended as a slight; you could tell he was going to be a player even then! Also, physically he was very big as a teenager, standing out among the rest of us. Strangely, he appeared to stop growing as he matured, necessitating him having to rely more on his not inconsiderable ability. While he was young, his footballing talent, coupled with his formidable physique, meant he was outstanding even among the best young players in London. Having been an early teammate of his, it wasn't a surprise that he went on to have the career that he did.

Inevitably, we attracted interest from professional clubs. It was rumoured at the time that Arsenal were looking to sign the whole team. Initially, this was a prospect that interested me, but with most of the side already fixed up with other London teams, nothing came of it. Even back then, the bigger clubs in the capital were very adept at poaching players once they had made headlines at schoolboy level. Some things never change! Unsurprisingly, playing for London and Surrey schoolboys put an increased level of focus on me, in the process opening the door to the possibility of a career in football. With this now a serious career prospect, my parents started taking more of an active involvement in my future. A keen sportsman himself, my father understandably liked the idea of a professional career in football, but my mother held firm, insisting that I complete my education first.

Even more so than it is today, football was a precarious occupation, and at 15 years of age there was no way of knowing what the future would hold. Things are very different now, with the massive financial rewards offered to youngsters often mitigating the level of risk, but that was not the case back then. In today's game, clubs will have already long earmarked the players they are interested in as youngsters, and probably already signed them up by this point. From a young age, players progress through the youth teams of the club of their choice. Their futures are already mapped out, accompanied by the prospect of an even more lucrative career should they eventually make the grade at a higher level.

At this time, the question of my actual position on

the pitch would become an issue. I played centre forward for the London district team, scoring a number of goals, but for London and Surrey I was often positioned at left-back, probably because I was left footed. Eventually, I settled at left-back. My reasoning was that there was less competition for places, as obviously the majority of players are right footed. Determined to not be hindered by a lack of versatility in this regard, I spent hours practising with my right foot, first in the streets of London against a convenient wall, and later against the wall at The Valley after I had joined Charlton Athletic. My right peg did gradually improve, but my left foot was always the stronger of the two.

My attacking instincts remained with me. As my skills developed and my career progressed, my speciality became that of an attacking full-back. Looking back, I don't think it's arrogant to say that I was ahead of my time in this respect. I developed good relationships with many of the left wingers I played with, in particular John Meredith, first at Gillingham and again at Bournemouth. I would overlap on the outside when they had the ball, they would play me in, and I would cross the ball near the byline for our forwards to attack. This worked particularly well at Bournemouth whenever Ted MacDougall was on the pitch, as he relied on a supply of crosses for him to attack. With Terry Gulliver on the other flank providing a good service as well, this created some excellent attacking options, but more about this later.

We needed a plan if I was going to fulfil my ambition of becoming a professional footballer while also keeping my mum happy. I knew that there were several clubs who were interested in me. Crystal Palace, Chelsea, Charlton and Brighton had all kept tabs at some point, not forgetting Arsenal from my time with London schools. Arsenal was an obvious consideration as an established First Division side, but being based in north London, Highbury wasn't the easiest place to get to. Chelsea had probably the best junior setup – but again, they were based in north London. The more southerly Crystal Palace was more convenient, but they were in the Third Division at that time, and therefore a less enticing prospect.

Charlton made contact after watching me play for Surrey against Kent, offering myself and my teammate, Trevor Wales, a trial. Following numerous discussions both with my parents and representatives from several of the aforementioned clubs, it was Charlton who won out, coming up with a plan that was agreeable to all parties. Peter Croker, an ex-player and head of youth recruitment at the time, persuaded me to join their youth squad. Despite being just 15 years of age, I took this all in my stride. It was an exciting prospect, but it came with a structured forward path, which kept my feet firmly on the ground and my parents happy as an added bonus.

As a sweetener for my mother, Peter managed to arrange for me to work and study to train as a design civil engineer at a local company, G A Harvey & Co, whose premises were a five-minute walk away from the ground. Initially I would be registered as an amateur, training in the evenings with the youth team while working full time. On top of this, I would attend college for one day and two evenings per week, at which time I would be studying for my Ordinary National Certificate in design engineering. Then, on Saturday mornings I would play for Charlton.

In those days there was no under 21 or development squad – just the first team, reserves, A-team, junior team and Robins (otherwise known as the reserve junior team). My debut for the Robins in the Woolwich League Division 2 couldn't have gone much better – a 12-0 win against ROF Apprentices on 6th September 1958, at the age of 15. Those kinds of scorelines weren't uncommon; in February 1959 we won another game 10-3 (I even scored!). Having impressed, I played a couple of matches for the juniors in the South East Counties League, before dividing my time reasonably evenly between the juniors and the Robins in the following season. For 1960/61, I became more of a permanent member of the juniors, playing 26 out of 28 matches. This was in addition to a stint in the FA Youth Cup, our run ended by a 4-1 defeat at West Ham (who included Martin Peters and Brian Dear in their lineup) in front of a crowd of over 2,000. Edging closer to the first-team picture, I also played a few games for the 'A' team in the Aetolian League.

Getting to The Valley and work involved a lot of travelling, which included a daily train journey from my home in Dulwich to London Bridge. I would then head on down to Charlton, where on exiting I turned left to work and right to the ground – simple but tiring. Plus, of course, I then had to go back again on the way home! Travelling like this became a real issue. After a couple of years of making the same journey, I decided to purchase a scooter. At the time this was a very popular means of transport, especially in London with its busy roads. What I didn't realise was that I needed permission from the club to use a scooter. For a few weeks, I parked outside the toilet by the club car park, leaving my helmet and clothing there. Looking back, I can't believe I did this, but I was young and perhaps more than a little bit foolish and naïve!

My new mode of transport was brought to a quick end by an accident on my scooter. While I was on the way back from a game of ten-pin bowling in Streatham with a girlfriend, a car unexpectedly pulled out in front of me on a one-way street. The subsequent coming-together resulted in a hospital visit in order to have some stitches on my chin. To make matters worse, I had been chosen to play in the first team at Plymouth Argyle on the following Saturday. This would have been my debut as a part-time professional. As this accident occurred only a few days before the match, I had to pull out of the game. Judging by the verbal blasting I got from the manager and one of the directors, the club weren't too impressed with me! Needless to say, I walked away with my ears burning and tail between my legs. The scooter was sold, and I was fined by the club. Somehow, the newspapers got hold of a very different story. Apparently I had fallen down some stairs, badly cutting my face and had to spend the match in hospital. Perhaps we'll never know the truth!

-

The normal process for a youngster to become part of a football club in those days was to join a club's 'ground staff'. On reflection this was a strange title, as it had very little to do with working in the ground. The ground staff boys were pretty much slave labour, as apart from their ground-based responsibilities – which included sweeping the stands after a match and cleaning the dressing room after training – they cleaned the players' boots, trainers and other gear. After training, all the kit would be thrown into the middle of the dressing room floor, along with the footwear, where it would be scooped up by one of the apprentices in readiness for the next day's training session. On match days, the routine would involve arriving about an hour or so before kick-off at home matches and laying out the kits, including boots, ready for the players' arrival. After this, they would be expected to be available pre-match to provide them with anything they needed. Post-match, they were expected to collect the kit and clean the changing room – not a very glamorous proposition!

The ground staff boys were normally aged between 15 and 17. If retained beyond this point, they would then be offered a professional contract at 18. Since I was registered as an amateur, I didn't have to do all the mundane tasks that the ground staff boys were forced to complete, and I'm glad of that. I definitely think I got the better deal by having an apprenticeship outside of football – which even then was a very unusual arrangement – and being able to become a part-time professional before ultimately becoming full time. Strangely, there was very little animosity from the other juniors over my arrangement and the perks that came with it, other than being nicknamed 'Lord Muck'! While unique in this regard, I wasn't by any means the only one who had this kind of setup. There were a few other part-time professionals in the game, mainly at semi-professional clubs like Wimbledon (who later turned full-time professional in 1964) and Kingstonian. However, it's worth noting that this was a time of 'shamateurs', where some players were officially of 'amateur' status, but received expenses for their troubles – sometimes quite considerable amounts.

I could have signed for a number of high-profile 'amateur' teams based in and around London who showed an interest. Sutton United were one, although I ruled them out due to the distance I'd need to travel. Dulwich Hamlet was another possibility – they were just round the corner, and I was well acquainted with them, since I played some matches for South London schools at their ground. However, in contrast to other 'amateur' sides, they didn't pay their players a penny, not even expenses. To be honest though, I didn't like the idea of playing purely as an amateur; I wanted a career, whether in football or elsewhere.

Ultimately, I was impressed with the approach and friendliness of Charlton, whose outlook I'm glad to say still exists within the club to this day. In some ways I was hedging my bets, keeping my mother happy by continuing to work, earning a salary and achieving academic qualifications, all while doing my best to make it as a professional footballer. I was spinning a lot of plates, but ultimately it all paid off.

TWO

WELCOME TO PROFESSIONAL FOOTBALL!

After playing in a number of games as an amateur – notably a 2-0 defeat against Chelsea at The Valley in the London Challenge Cup, courtesy of two goals from England striker Bobby Tambling – in 1961, at the age of 18, I signed as a part-time professional on a one-year contract. The terms of this were as follows: £6 a week during the season, and £5 a week in the off season, with a £2 bonus for a win and £1 for a draw (all this accompanying the £7 a week I was still earning as an apprentice design engineer at Harvey).

I felt pretty well-off for the first time, and indeed after a few months I purchased my first car, a baby blue Volkswagen Beetle, and obtained a full driving licence. As well as making me the envy of my mates, travelling to training became less problematic – there were to be no more scooter-related mishaps! At this stage of both my careers, I was growing up very quickly, and realised that a big decision was on the horizon: whether to continue as a part-time professional footballer along with my other job or commit to playing football on a full-time basis. It was a difficult decision to make, especially considering my mum and dad's opposing viewpoints on this.

Even though I was technically a part-time professional and not yet training with the first team, I was eventually noticed. After some injuries to first-team players, I was selected for the first team. And the match that was to serve as the site of my league debut? Against Liverpool at Anfield, no less!

Considering the evocations of the likes of Bill Shankly, Bob Paisley et al that immediately spring to mind whenever the word 'Liverpool' is mentioned, not to mention the club's illustrious history, it's easy to forget that they once found themselves in the old Second Division for a substantial stretch of time, having been relegated from the First Division at the close of the 1953/54 season. Sitting pretty at the top of the table, Liverpool were already confirmed as league winners. Before the season came to an end however, they had to play host to a Charlton Athletic side bearing yours truly as part of its starting line-up for the final game of the year.

While Liverpool are undoubtedly the more illustrious of the two clubs, at this point it was actually Charlton who had the most recent experience at the highest level. Having spent 15 years in the First Division before dropping down at the end of the 1956/57 season, their stay in the Second Division would last a fair bit longer, not returning to the top flight until 1986. Even so, we were definitely the underdogs, being two games away from an eventual 15th place finish.

Having played Preston North End on Saturday 28th April at Deepdale (a 2-0 loss), we stayed up in Lancashire for a couple of nights. This made sense, since the Liverpool game was on the following Monday evening: 30th April 1962, with a 7.15pm kick off. Under the Anfield floodlights, I would make my debut against the likes of Emlyn Hughes, Roger Hunt, Ian St John, Ian Callaghan, Peter Thompson and the rest of their squad of international stalwarts. Not too much pressure then! It was the first time I had travelled with the first team. Even so, I didn't have an inkling that I would actually be playing. There wasn't much build-up; I travelled, and on the day of the game I was told by the manager, Frank Hill, that I would be playing.

Unsurprisingly, the prospect of facing off against a team of this stature – at 19 years of age, no less – was pretty terrifying. Still, the Charlton senior players were great with me, notably Mike Bailey, Marvin Hinton and John Hewie. Their advice was straightforward enough: go out and enjoy it! My response? "Oh yeah, sure!" 34,327 spectators at Anfield, in fine voice and hoping to see their side clinch the title, was a bit of a different prospect to playing in front of 100 or so in the reserves or third XI at The Valley, or on pitch two at Streatham Common in London on a Sunday morning with my mates! (I wasn't really supposed to be playing, but anyway…)

As you would expect when recalling a formative life experience, I can picture the occasion pretty clearly. Having arrived at the ground some two hours before kick-off, we were met by the obligatory barrage of verbal abuse dished out by the home supporters as we disembarked the coach. Before getting changed, myself and the rest of the squad went out to look at the pitch. The floodlights were only switched on at about half their usual brightness, which created a strange atmosphere amid the setting sun. Having seen us, the ten thousand or so Liverpool supporters who had already taken their places unleashed a torrent of whistling, which let me tell you, in the murky light was more than a bit sinister! With that, we all scurried back into the dressing room. For me at least, this didn't help; the silence in the changing room, standing out in stark contrast to the roar of the crowd outside, was far more effective at giving me the collywobbles!

In keeping with the gamesmanship that some sides choose to employ, there was no heating in the dressing room. Plus, they only gave us one football to kick about before the game. It was all part of the tactics! Even so, it wasn't considered much of a deal. Back in those days, there was no structured pre-match warm-up in the manner that you see before matches today; you just got changed into your kit, ran out and kicked off. Waiting around in the changing room for the signal to go out was something I recall as being very daunting. No one spoke, as the players were all going through their own pre-match rituals: left boot on first, kissing the number on the back of the shirt, or suchlike. Mine was to warm my feet up in the bath before putting my socks and boots on, and then kick the ball against the wall of the bath area to get a feel of the ball. This was a routine I did throughout my career, assuming there was enough room – at some grounds, the space available was very limited, even at some of the bigger clubs.

Looking back, the Charlton squad were one of the quietest groups of players before a match that I played with. The senior players were generally pretty laid back (notably Hewie and Hinton), and the younger players subsequently looked up to them and tried to emulate their demeanour. One of the few exceptions to this was skipper Mike Bailey, who was fairly vocal both on and off the pitch. His attitude was superb, and he was a great leader. One word from him was enough to make you do what you were told. He and Frank Hill worked well together – it was him who gave Frank the nickname 'Tiger'. This came about because when Frank got annoyed, he would make a growling sound. Frank loved it – he definitely didn't discourage the nickname's use!!

In the first half we defended the Kop end, from which the home supporters made their presence known. We conceded a corner a few minutes in, and the noise was incredible. It was little wonder they were at the top of the table when they had this level of support to count on – that, and the quality of players in their team, of course! Somehow, we came in at half time with the game still goalless. Then, the unexpected happened: we took the lead through Bailey, who put one away on the 60-minute mark. Sadly, this would not prove to be a dream debut for me: Liverpool came back to equalise through future World Cup winner Roger Hunt just before the 90-minute mark, and Alan A'Court notched the winner with seconds left. Having been a mere two minutes away from spoiling Liverpool's title party, we slipped up at the death. Anfield was a hard place to come to at the best of times, with their last home defeat occurring back on New Years' Eve in a 4-3 reverse against Middlesbrough, which speaks volumes about Charlton's performance. Regardless, we weren't to be party poopers, as the Liverpool team were presented with the Second Division championship trophy.

The full line-ups for the match were as follows:

Liverpool – Furnell, Byrne, Moran, Milne, Yeats,
    Leishman, Callaghan, Hunt, St John, Melia, A'Court.
Charlton – Duff, Sewell, Stocks, Hewie, Tocknell, Bailey,
    Lawrie, Matthews, Leary, Edwards, Kinsey.

It was a disappointing result, but what a debut for me – a far cry from the comparative quiet of the 'A' team in the Aetolian League against the likes of Cray Wanderers and Bexley in front of a few hundred spectators. Among the newspaper cuttings that my family have kept safely stowed away, one briefly summarises my contribution as follows:

Brian Tocknell played at centre-half, with John Hewie at right-half, and 19-year-old David Stocks making his debut at left-back. The youngster played a great game.

That'll do! Not bad for my first appearance. Little did I know, this would not be my last visit to Anfield in a playing capacity.

-

Another game that stands out from around this time was in the Kent Challenge Cup against our arch-rivals, Millwall, at the Den – another intimidating venue, albeit for different reasons (I'm not sure why either team participated in this competition, as neither are actually based in Kent!). It wasn't a league game – indeed, against most other opposition it would be treated more like a friendly, but that certainly wasn't going to be the case here! Playing at left-back against their flying right winger, Joey Broadfoot, proved to be quite a challenge, but I think I coped well. He was a cult hero, loved by the crowd for being a fast and aggressive little winger – quite typical for those days.

When the ball was played out to him, naturally as the left full-back I would be responsible for marking him. His tactic would be to knock the ball past you and accelerate, mainly on the outside, leaving you in his wake. He would then cross the ball into the penalty area for the oncoming Millwall forwards – a fairly simple tactic, but an effective one. As a local lad he had a bit of a reputation: a typical cockney, but as I got to know him he proved to be a real character.

One word of advice dished out by the other players when at The Den – apart from to try to give Joey a few kicks – was to avoid collecting the ball from the crowd if it landed among them. If you made the mistake of wading in to fish it out yourself, aside from the verbal abuse that would be volleyed your way, the likelihood of being on the receiving end of a right-hander from one of their supporters was high. There was no love lost between the two clubs, or indeed any club who found themselves playing against Millwall, especially at The Den. Some things never change!

As it happened, this wouldn't be my last contact with Joey. Along with a number of other players, in 1967 – by which point I was a Bournemouth player – I embarked on a programme of study for my Football Association Coaching Certificate at Lilleshall. This was a one-week residential course for the preliminary award at the cost of 7/6d, followed a year later by a two-week course to get the full badge. Hearing that I was to be in attendance, Joey made contact and offered to drive us both there. I accepted, but quickly regretted it. He turned up in a convertible sports car with the roof off and drove like a lunatic all the way there. Most of the attendees on the course were either ex or current players, and it turned out to be a lot of fun, with a great feeling of camaraderie that carried on for a number of years, especially on the nights out. I managed to pass my preliminary award, and the following year gained my full badge, at which time I was one of the youngest, at the age of 25, to achieve the full award.

I went into the 1962/63 season – my first as a full-time professional – determined to nail down a regular starting place in the Charlton first team. This proved to be difficult, as despite being a Second Division team, we still had a number of full internationals sprinkled throughout the line-up – Marvin Hinton, Mike Bailey, Eddie Firmani and John Hewie among them – and a strong back-up squad. Breaking through was going to be a tall order. This was a time of transition for me: it was a huge challenge moving from playing in a junior team to being in the first team with first team players, some of whom played internationally. Saying this, I thought I coped very well, as training full time ultimately helped me become fitter and stronger. I also finally stopped playing with my mates on Sunday mornings: it probably wasn't worth the grief I'd get for picking up an injury!

Of course, not every game could be at Anfield, but there were still some huge crowds at Second Division matches. One highlight from my first full season was against Stoke City at The Valley early on in the 1962/63 season. The main reason that this game stands out was the inclusion in the Stoke line-up of a certain Stanley Matthews, who despite being at the relatively advanced age of 46 (having re-signed for Stoke during the previous season following a 14-year stint at Blackpool), went on to make 31 appearances that campaign. At this point he played in short bursts – he would demand the ball from teammates when it suited him. If he didn't want the ball, he would simply turn his back on them! Whenever any of the Charlton players attempted to tackle him, the crowd showed their dissatisfaction by booing us for daring to take out their superstar. Not that our attempts did us any good – we lost 3-0, with Keith Bebbington, Jackie Mudie and Bill Asprey the scorers.

My first game that season – my first as a full-time professional – was a 2-1 victory at home to Leicester (featuring Gordon Banks in goal) in the League Cup on 2nd October. My first league appearance came four days later in a 3-2 victory at home to Walsall, Brian Ord and Lenny Glover the scorers (plus an own goal). After dropping out of the team for a spell, I returned on 24th November for an away tie against Huddersfield, which we lost 2-0. I played four more games, sadly also all defeats, falling down against Middlesbrough, Derby, Swansea and Chelsea. That final one featured my former London schools teammate, Terry Venables, along with England goalkeeper Peter Bonetti.

As it turned out, Venables recognised me from our time playing together as schoolboys. During this time, I had been preferred in the starting line-up to his mate, Allan Harris (later his assistant at Barcelona) – apparently something he never forgot. He couldn't resist twisting the knife as Chelsea beat us 4-1 at The Valley, saying something along the lines of "You're still no better than Allan Harris!"

After another spell out of the team, my return on 19th January at Southampton was curtailed on the 57th minute when a snowstorm put paid to play (irritatingly, we were 1-0 up at the time). Followed by another seven appearances (including a 1-0 home victory against Cardiff in the FA Cup, another defeat at the hands of Chelsea and Venables in the following round, and a nine-goal thriller in the 6-3 home victory against Plymouth), that was to be my lot for the season, which saw Charlton finish in 20th. It would prove to be the most appearances I made in a single season during my time at Charlton.

The following year, the team turned it around, ultimately attaining a fourth-place finish. However, they did this largely without me. Having spent the majority of the season playing for the reserves in the Football Combination and Metropolitan League (which the A-team was now playing in, having withdrawn from the Aetolian League at the end of the 1961/62 season), it wasn't until 4th January 1964 that I made my first appearance. In fairness, though, it was a good place to start: in the FA Cup at Upton Park against West Ham. Featuring future World Cup winners Bobby Moore and Geoff Hurst, they comfortably dominated the game, running out 3-0 winners (Hurst being joined on the score sheet by Peter Brabrook and John Sissons). It didn't help that I was playing at right-back on this occasion – not really my position. People have sometimes asked whether I, as a young pro, ever got starstruck playing against those types of players. The answer is no, not really. I would always do my best to play my usual game, and there was never anyone who would cause me to get excited; I just did my job. From game to game, the majority of my focus was on the other team's right winger, whoever that might be.

My next game two weeks later – away at Huddersfield – was another abandonment, this time due to fog. My luck didn't get much better, with my other three matches all ending in defeat: 2-1 at home to Leyton Orient, 2-1 away at Huddersfield, and a 2-0 reverse at home to a Don Revie-helmed Leeds. Facing off against the likes of Billy Bremner, Jack Charlton, Johnny Giles and Norman Hunter, this could nonetheless have had a different outcome had Dennis Edwards not smashed his penalty wide after being brought down by Charlton in the 80th minute. We may have already been down to two goals from Alan Peacock, but we could have run them closer.

1964/65 was another late start for me as I struggled to displace Kinsey, although happily this time it arrived in the form of a victory: 1-0 away at Huddersfield on 24th October courtesy of a 77th-minute strike from Eddie Firmani. This commenced another mini run in the team: winning 3-0 at home to Coventry, before a three-game losing run: an embarrassing 1-0 home defeat to Fourth Division Bradford in the League Cup; 2-1 away at Cardiff, and 3-1 home to Preston. This was arrested by a 1-1 draw away at Ipswich, followed by a 3-2 victory at home to Plymouth the following week.

From there, my appearances became more sporadic: 3-3 at home to Portsmouth on 19th December; 1-1 against Rotherham on 6th February, and a 2-0 reverse at Norwich in the following week, before being recalled to the first team for the final two games of the season: a 2-1 victory away at Middlesbrough, and a 2-1 reverse at Maine Road against Manchester City that saw us cement 18th position in the table. With the quality of players in and around our team during this time (one notable addition was Firmani, who had returned after a spell in Italy playing for Sampdoria, Internazionale and Genoa), these fluctuating fortunes served as a stark reminder of just how difficult to get out of the old Second Division it was.

This section pretty neatly sums up my time at Charlton: in and out of the first team, and at the mercy of Kinsey's fitness!

-

a clear structure to the different teams at
I touched upon earlier, the first team played
_____ ____ _____d Division; the reserves played in the Football
Combination; the third team in the Aetolian League and
later the Metropolitan League; the Juniors, who competed
in the South-East Counties League; and the Juniors'
second team, known as the Robins, who played in the
Minor Division of the Woolwich & District League. Since
my appearances in the first team were pretty sporadic, I
ended up flitting around these teams a fair bit. Was it ever
distracting, not knowing where I was playing from one
week to the next? Not really – I grew up playing alongside
a lot of these players, so we were used to each other. I
actually enjoyed playing in the Aetolian League the most:
it was against a number of semi-professionals, and there
were plenty of good, young players.

The first team itself could be a bit intimidating,
composed as it was from several internationals, but
generally, Charlton was – and is – a very friendly club. The
supporters were generally very patient, in contrast to other
clubs, whose support would be very much conditional on
how you played.

-

A number of players stand out from my time at the club.
Our goalkeeper, Willie Duff, played 230 games for Charlton
after signing from Hearts. He was a fine keeper, if difficult
to understand at times with his strong Scottish accent, so
communication was not his strong point, especially in the

heat of the battle. The two full-backs in particular also remain in the memory. On the right was John Hewie, who despite being born in South Africa, played for Scotland at international level thanks to a long-lost relative of Scottish extraction. He seemed to have extraordinarily long legs, and very seldom got beaten by the opposition winger. He sometimes played in central defence, and made over 500 appearances for the club from the '50s to the mid '60s, along with 19 appearances for Scotland.

On the left was Brian Kinsey, a very solid and consistent left-back with 411 appearances to his name over a 14-year period, having made his debut in the 1956/57 season. He sometimes played further forward on the left wing, which would enable me to be slotted in at left-back. There was some rivalry between us – he was older and quite cold towards me. This didn't bother me, as I understood his attitude; I was the one trying to take his place, so it's natural that we weren't best mates. As it happened, he didn't have much to worry about, as I only got into the team if he played on the left wing!

Most of the other players wanted me in the team and Brian on the wing – Mike Bailey in particular was very outspoken about it. However, my relationship with manager Hill wasn't great, plus I think Kinsey preferred to play left-back, and with Len Glover developing as a left winger, I was gradually being eased out of the left-back position. Eventually, I only played if Kinsey was injured, which wasn't very often. It was unfortunate, but that's professional football – it can be a tough game.

Other notable players in the squad at that time

included two England internationals: the aforementioned Bailey, and Marvin Hinton, who were without doubt two of the best players I played with. Both were memorable for different reasons: Bailey was all aggression and enthusiasm, quick to tackle, pass the ball and press forward to midfield, with his positive play garnering him 22 goals from 169 appearances for Charlton. Before his high-profile transfer to Wolverhampton Wanderers in 1966, he was capped for England twice: against the USA in 1964 and Wales in 1965. Moreover, he was a natural leader and captain, and a superb player with a great attitude to matches. He was the same in training: the ultimate professional.

Marvin Hinton was a cultured centre-back, a class act with 145 first team appearances to his name from 1957 to 1963, before moving to Chelsea and playing in the old First Division. Everything came easy for him; he cruised through training and matches. Another class player was Eddie Firmani at centre forward, who actually had three spells at the club: 1951-55, 1963-65 and 1966-68, making a total of 177 appearances and 89 goals. He spent some time in Italian football, as well as representing the Italian international side, despite having been born and raised in South Africa. He was an interesting character, not only due to his background, but also because of his attitude to matches and training, which was vastly different to the rest of us – the experience he had in Italian football being brought to training.

He was very serious in his approach to playing, doing a number of extra exercises to stretch his body, and was fully committed to the physical side of things; he was a true athlete. His ball work was exemplary, and as a centre forward his build-up play was brilliant, with total control of the ball, and his finishing in front of goal was excellent. The only problem he had was that physically he wasn't strong enough to consistently perform at a high level throughout the season, which resulted in him being unable to cope with the pace of the Second Division. Regardless, his attitude and work ethic impressed me, and having spent time with him, his influence changed my attitude towards the game for the better.

Then there were Keith Peacock and Len Glover – my best mates. Similar ages to me, we had come through the ranks at the club together, and Keith was actually the best man at my first wedding. They were both to stay on at the club for some time after I left, Glover making 196 appearances, scoring 24 goals from 1962 to 1968, then going on to play for Leicester City. Keith became a legend at Charlton, making 567 appearances with 107 goals from 1962 to 1979, and is still to this day involved with the club.

Even though Keith is correctly regarded as a legend at Charlton for the amount of appearances he made, I don't feel that he gets the credit he deserves from the wider footballing community. Other than Ted MacDougall, he was the best that I have played with. His son Gavin went on to have a similarly great career – in addition to spells at Gillingham, Bournemouth and Charlton (nearly a clean sweep of my clubs!), he also starred at Queens Park Rangers, Newcastle and Chelsea.

–

Professional football at league level nowadays is far more scientific and structured than it used to be, with training and match preparation in particular being vastly different – I'm not sure how I would cope now! To give you an idea of how much things have changed, it might be helpful to tell you what the routine was like at Charlton.

A normal training day would take place at The Valley – we had no training ground or other facilities to go to. It would start with a few laps around the pitch, with groups of four running on the gravel for about 30 minutes or so: full laps, half laps whole sides, i.e. from one corner flag at one end of the pitch to the other. Earlier in the week we would also run up and down the steep terracing opposite the main stand – very sophisticated!

There was a small gymnasium available under the main stand where we sometimes did weight training. We weren't given instructions on what to lift and for how often – we were left to our own devices. The full squad would consist of twenty or so players, and after the main running drills we would split into two groups: one would go to the gym for weight training, and the other would again run up and down the terracing, then we would switch round. This all culminated in a small-sided game out the back of the main stand on the gravel, which on match days was used as a car park.

The make-up of the teams was interesting owing to the different nationalities of the squad, which was quite diverse for the era, encompassing citizens of England, Scotland, Ireland, South Africa and Italy. The manager was Scottish, as was the trainer, Jock Basford. When it was time for the training match, which would take place in the car park at the front of the main stand, Hill would come out in his suit and tie, put his boots on, tuck his trousers into his socks, and join in with the game. He would want his own team to be made up of all the non-English players, preferably the Scots, and we would have an international game that Jock would referee. You would think we were playing in the World Cup, what with the seriousness that the players approached proceedings – fights breaking out in these England vs Rest of the World clashes were not uncommon. The winning team were treated to a bottle of Coca-Cola each – there were none of those energy drinks or protein shakes back then! After training, a few of us would then head off to Don's Café for a rewarding sausage sandwich and a cup of tea. This was conveniently located next to the Charlton railway station, so after this I would catch the train to Waterloo, head down to West Norwood and walk home to Dulwich.

As we now had time on our hands – with no training in the afternoon – some of the players used to coach football in local schools. Having been accustomed to working eight-hour days, with my apprenticeship at Harvey's still fresh in the memory, I felt at a loose end in the afternoons, prompting me to join my colleagues in coaching. It was at this time that I purchased a car, a little Volkswagen Beetle, which made me more mobile and able to get to the school and home again.

Coaching in schools was a financially rewarding occupation, as at the time there was a shortage of teachers in the local schools, especially in and around London. The teaching was very academically driven, but there was a shortage of staff available to teach sport, with generations missing following the war. The coaching proved to be an interesting experience – I was in my early twenties, and the kids were about 15 or 16, so there wasn't a massive age gap. The pupils would be transported to playing fields outside London, which could take as long as an hour's drive on a coach, so most of our time was spent sitting at the back, monitoring the behaviour of the pupils. With the lengthy travel durations, it would only leave us with enough time for a very short football match. More time was spent as a coach driver than as an actual trainer.

-

Pre-match rituals were quite personal, and the changing room was usually pretty quiet, although whether this was the case generally depended on the mood of the manager and captain. There was an air of contemplation before matches – we didn't go out on to the pitch before a match like they do now to warm up. If you did, it was only to inspect the pitch, especially for those players that had an extra bonus in their contract for crowd numbers, hoping for a good attendance to give them additional money. There was no official warm-up – the closest I got was to heat my feet up in the small baths, then rub oil into my legs. Once dressed in the full kit, I would then take a football into the bathroom area and gently kick a ball up against a wall and jog a little on the spot, then do a few stretches and head out onto the pitch.

Once out there, I would do a few sprints, and then exchange a couple of passes with my teammates, after which the game would start. I probably did more than most, with some doing nothing at all – no wonder there were so many muscle strains in those days! I do recall that some of the strikers would take a football in the changing room and knock it against their heads in preparation for heading the ball. As we had to walk past the away team's changing room door to get to the home team changing room, some of the defenders would give their door a kick for luck. This was also done later on at Bournemouth, but that was because the two changing rooms had an adjoining door, so it was used for a little knockabout in the hope that it would annoy or intimidate the opposition.

All in, I made 31 appearances in the first team between the 1961/62 and 1964/65 seasons. The main factor in preventing me from adding to this total was that I relied on the first-choice left-back, Brian Kinsey, to either get injured or suffer from a loss of form. While Kinsey was an excellent player who went on to be a Charlton legend, this didn't at all lessen my frustration at not having played more games. Having tasted first team football on such a prominent stage, my appetite had been whetted for more.

However, all things must come to an end, as I found out in May 1965. Having played in the last league game of the season (a 2-1 reverse against Manchester City at Maine Road), we travelled back to London on the overnight train.

Previously, I had been led to believe that come the end of the season, I would be offered a new two-year contract, and thereafter seriously considered for a regular first team place. There was indeed a letter waiting for me when I got back – however, rather than confirming my new contract, it was informing me that I had been given a free transfer. Me and my family were mortified. So after seven years, having joined Charlton from school at the age of 15, and progressing through the juniors up to first team squad, playing 31 first team games in the process, my Charlton career was over.

At this stage, aged 22, I was unsure what my future held. To my mind, I was now without a club, and seemingly without a footballing future. Since I hadn't neglected my education, I even considered looking for a career away from football. My decision, however, was made for me when Freddie Cox, the manager of Gillingham, asked if I would be interested in joining them. Gillingham, playing in the Third Division, always had a link with Charlton, as they are fairly close to each other geographically, plus I knew one or two of their players from previous pre-season friendlies. Somewhat abruptly, my time at Charlton had come to an end.

INTERLUDE

When I first signed for Charlton at the age of 17, David had just signed professional terms, having been part-time. We became quite good friends as we were playing in the reserves a lot together, as well as in the first team. He always came across as an intelligent fellow – a thinking full-back, a good size for one in those days. He had a great left foot, and was always calm and classy on the ball. He was the best man at my wedding in July 1965, and three weeks later I was the best man at his!

When you've been through a period of time together, particularly when you're young and you're trying to climb the ladder to get into the first team, you have the camaraderie. This is notably the case in football, with the banter that goes on, you lived or died by how you could handle it in the dressing room, because it could be quite ruthless. Those were special days – we were together for three years. We could go 15-20 years without making much contact, and pick up where we left off. You can link up with a former player who you've been friends with, and it's like the time hasn't gone by. I think that's the way it is in football.

It was a bit of a surprise when David was given a free transfer – I don't think anyone expected that. It didn't help that Brian Kinsey had dropped back to become a full-back. Being in his mid 20s and established, it was always going to be difficult for David to get past him. If David had been able to remain at Charlton for another year or so, he would have been a regular player – he was just unfortunate that he had Brian in front of him, who very seldom got injured, so the pathway wasn't there for his position.

It all happened very quickly – from being great mates together, he went off to Gillingham. Really, I would say he was unfortunate to be given a free transfer. He phoned me up to tell me, and I was shocked – just didn't see it coming. In those days, you were told at the last minute – you got a letter in the post usually. Nowadays, players would already be saying "Look, if you don't give me a contract now, I'll be looking for a club", whereas players then didn't have that sort of power. You would be more happy to see what contract was offered to you, so people wouldn't know until they got the letter through the door. I think it was the second Saturday in May when they used to have to send you the letter, which was quite ruthless – there was no discussion with the manager, you just got the letter! It's a pity he wasn't able to stay on longer or change his position. He's a good man, and was an intelligent player.

Keith Peacock
Teammate at Charlton Athletic

THREE

A SHORT SPELL IN KENT

I met Freddie Cox for the first time in the corridor outside the dressing rooms at The Den following Charlton's last game of the season: the Kent Challenge Cup final against Millwall. By this point, I had already been told that I was being released, so I wasn't entirely sure why I was playing. Regardless, it was a good opportunity to put myself in the shop window, and maybe Frank Hill felt a little guilty about releasing me. I know that a number of supporters and players had expressed their surprise at my impending departure, which was comforting to hear.

My feelings on hearing that Gillingham were interested in signing me were mixed: on the one hand I was still disappointed to be leaving Charlton, but on the other I was happy that another club wanted me. My confidence had been dented by the experience of being let go by Charlton, and knowing that I had another option on the cards went some way to restoring it. Following a number of conversations with my parents and some of my former Charlton teammates – who generally expressed amazement that I had been released – I decided to continue my career in football.

At the end of the 1964/65 season, I signed a two-year contract with the Gills, and moved away from my beloved Charlton Athletic. It was a sad occasion, but a great opportunity to become a regular first teamer and full-time professional. At the age of 22, it was something my football career needed. Moreover, with Gillingham not required to pay a transfer fee, I was able to negotiate a decent wage and signing-on fee for myself – there were no agents in those days!

Dropping down to the Third Division was a definite culture shock. The football was far more physical than I was used to, and Gillingham played very differently to how Charlton did in the Second Division, especially under the management of Freddie. By necessity, my playing style had to change. At Charlton, as a full-back I would jockey the attacking opposition player and try to steal the ball from him, then pass it on to one of our midfield players – invariably an international player, who would then provide the craft. At Gillingham, I was encouraged to tackle as soon as possible, get the ball and pass it up to one of our forwards – Brian Gibbs or Brian Yeo – bypassing the midfield in the process. Plus, I was expected to make runs on the outside of our forward players to provide crosses for the strikers in the box. Obviously this was very physically demanding, but I was young and fit, and immensely enjoyed this style of play.

Playing for Gillingham also introduced me to what has sometimes been described as the 'darker' side of professional football. I was expected to physically challenge the opposition – a polite way of dishing out a few kicks – with a number of Gills players obligingly introducing me to the tricks of the trade. It's fair to say that very few teams enjoyed their visit to Priestfield! This style of football back in the mid '60s was fairly common. The game in the lower leagues was very physical, and referees were far more relaxed about physical contact – very different to today's softies! Anybody showing pain from a tackle by writhing around on the floor would be told to get up and get on with the game – even by their own teammates – unless they were actually injured!

The nature of the game at this level was hammered home to me in one game where after misplacing a pass, a fellow defender made it clear to me in no certain terms (and with at least one expletive thrown in) that my job as a defender wasn't to pass it forward; it was to launch it up the field. I duly obliged. While this change of style pleased my teammates, a visiting friend from my Charlton days wondered aloud to me what had happened to my relatively cultured passing style. Needs must!

-

One of my first matches for the Gills was a friendly against my old club, Charlton – what a start! The banter on the pitch was interesting to say the least, especially from my old teammates, Keith Peacock, Len Glover and Billy

Bonds, but it started before the match even began when I walked into their dressing room to say hi. I received a barrage of good-natured abuse along the lines of, "You're in the wrong dressing room Stocksy, piss off." This carried on out onto the pitch throughout the game – it was all light-hearted, as we had been good mates. I think the game being a friendly made it easier for me emotionally, as leaving on a free transfer feels a bit like being sacked from your job, so inevitably you are full of mixed emotions towards your old team for a while.

Billy – or Bonzo, as he was known – was renowned for his fitness, although that didn't stop me taking it past him at one point. I can't remember exactly what words I used, but on running back a comment was made along the lines of "Have you lost your pace, Bonzo?" which he just smiled at. I actually sent him a copy of some photographic evidence of this happening. Needless to say, I never got a response, but what a great player he was. In my opinion he should have played for England – he was an incredible athlete, and a fan favourite both at The Valley and later at Upton Park. He would always give one hundred per cent.

Reflecting back, an incredible number of players came through the system at Charlton: the likes of Keith Peacock, Len Glover, Roy Matthews, Brian Kinsey, Marvin Hinton and Mike Bailey. These were recruited in the main by Peter Croker – the more high-profile London clubs, such as Chelsea, Arsenal, West Ham, Fulham and Tottenham, had their own scouts, and London during the '60s was a hotbed of football talent. Consequently, at schoolboy and junior level, the competition was very intense, and clubs were active in their recruitment of young players, as it saved them an awful lot of money in transfer fees.

-

Another game I recall from my early days for Gillingham was a League Cup tie away at Blackpool, where we got a lesson in not just football, but the darker side of the game of which we were supposedly so adept at. Blackpool were in the old First Division at the time, and among their ranks was a certain Alan Ball of England fame. It was a cold, wet evening, and Ball put on a good show of his pedigree. Accompanying this were some less than savoury tactics, which included a few late tackles and some uncomplimentary verbals inferring that our footballing abilities were of a questionable standard (this is very much the polite version!).

This was rather disappointing to witness from a player of his calibre. Besides, Gillingham were probably not the best team to have provoked, as we would always give as good as we got. I was not immune to his tactics, as he played on the right, which meant he came into my vicinity on several occasions. During one incident, he came steaming in with a late tackle while making a clearance, taking me down in the process – an action that went unobserved by the referee. I was able to gain retribution a few minutes later with a heavy tackle while going for the ball, which my teammates applauded, and even some of the Blackpool playing contingent appeared to be happy about. Game on, Mr Ball. He didn't come over to my side again after that!

The rest of the game didn't go quite so much in my favour: opportunities going forward proved limited, thanks to my opposing right-back being England international and Blackpool captain Jimmy Armfield, who even at this late stage of his career was an excellent player. A newspaper report confirmed our good performance as a team, describing how "full-backs Ralph Miller and David Stocks excelled themselves against people like former international Alan Ball", and admitting that we were ultimately "not disgraced". Perhaps the scoreline (a 5-2 defeat) was a little harsh, but the antics of Mr Ball unfortunately remain in the memory!

Another game that stands out is a home tie against Brighton, which we won 3-1. Reading an old match report from the game, it refers to the unusual formation Gillingham used: two strikers, and wingers playing deep. This would now be known as a 4-4-2 formation, so Freddie Cox was certainly ahead of his time when it came to sorting his team's playing style. I set up Yeo in the third minute with a cross, with Gibbs and Ron Newman finishing off the scoring.

During the course of the season, my form continued to improve, as playing first-team football on a regular basis had the effect of boosting my confidence. I was playing in a way that suited my strengths and I had a great relationship with the fans. During my time there, my style of play gradually changed – I became more aggressive and physical, some might say too much, but this was demanded from me by the management team, and I happily obliged.

We were constantly challenging near the top – we finished in sixth place overall – but probably not quite consistent enough for promotion. The Brighton victory was part of a three-match winning sequence that was immediately followed by two defeats. This kind of pattern wasn't uncommon: later, a four-game league unbeaten run (including a 4-0 battering of Oxford) was capped off by a 3-1 defeat at Exeter. We immediately followed this up with consecutive triumphs against Workington, Swindon and York, then won just once in our next ten games. Among this barren run were a few personal highlights and lowlights: I picked up the man of the match award in a 1-1 home draw against Peterborough, then saw a goal disallowed in a 4-2 home defeat to Reading, before missing a free kick to keep things square in a 2-1 loss at Shrewsbury.

The rest of the season was characterised by similar fluctuations in performance: we won three and lost four of the next seven games (two of which were back-to-back pastings: 5-2 at Southend and 6-1 at Walsall), before winning seven of our final nine games.

There were a few individual players at Gillingham that stood out to me, such as John Simpson, one of the best goalkeepers in the Third Division playing behind probably the best defence in the division. My full-back colleague was Ralph Miller, who arrived with me from Charlton, and was a very fit and aggressive defender. Funnily enough, our career paths would cross again, as he joined me at Bournemouth a couple of years after I signed for them. Clearly he missed me!

The central defenders were Jimmy White (also later to sign for Bournemouth) and Rod Taylor (another future Bournemouth player), both of whom arrived from one of manager Freddie Cox's previous clubs, Portsmouth. The forward line was led by Brian Gibbs and Brian Yeo, two hard-working goalscoring forwards. Together, they formed the basis of a very efficient team.

It came as a surprise when Cox, the manager who signed me from Charlton, left to take over at Bournemouth. Our new manager was Basil Hayward. None of us knew anything about him – indeed, his previous experience was all at non-league level, namely Yeovil and Bedford Town, and it quickly became clear that I was not his cup of tea. When he first arrived, he would watch us in training while still in his suit, tie and overcoat. His tone with the players was generally pretty critical, with no real encouragement. The senior players were not impressed, and coming from non-league to the Third Division, I felt it was a step too far for him. As regards his attitude towards me, I can't remember a constructive conversation I ever had with him relating to my role on and off the pitch. Regardless, I took no notice and concentrated on playing.

Towards the end of the season, rumours were rife that I would be leaving the club. My new playing style, which combined utilising my physicality with my natural playing skills, created a lot of interest from clubs higher up the league pyramid. There were rumours of interest from London clubs like Queens Park Rangers, Fulham and even Arsenal, but it soon became clear that I would be following Freddie Cox to Bournemouth, along with some of my teammates. Having missed just one out of 46 games and being voted player of the year by the supporters, it was quite a shock to be off so soon, but as they say, it's a funny old game!

The move to Bournemouth was not what I really wanted at the time, as I was playing regular first-team football, and had continued my side hustle of coaching at local schools, but I was simply told, "You're being transferred to Bournemouth, drive down and sort your contract out, we don't want you anymore. Goodbye." It was as blunt as that. I believe there were offers from two other clubs – Fulham and Bristol City – but back then, with no agents involved, the club did all the negotiating on my behalf. The transfer fee was agreed, and I was just told that it was Bournemouth I would be heading to.

I was withdrawn from the team for the last game of the season at Brentford, since Bournemouth didn't want me injured. It was a bit bizarre, as I had already played 45 games in the league (plus cup matches) without injury, but in those days that was the way it was; there was no agent to negotiate your contract, it was all down to you. With that, I was off, with Bournemouth's Charlie Crickmore moving the other way in part exchange.

I had learnt an awful lot during my one season at Gillingham. It was far removed from the Charlton way, with the players not being as gifted as their counterparts at my former club, but they more than made up for this with their tremendous will to win, and it was certainly more physical and competitive, even in training, where there were regular fights between players. Even with this competitive edge during the training sessions, they were still a lot of fun, with activities such as leapfrog and steeplechase taking on paramount importance, especially in view of the lack of training facilities – and they certainly didn't want us on the pitch, which was not in great condition anyway!

My previously moderate enthusiasm was given a jolt when I realised where Bournemouth was: on the south coast. Pretty much a holiday resort! I travelled down to meet with Cox to discuss my contract, and he painted a good picture of the club. Around this time, he was also trying to sign a few other members of the Gillingham team, such as Tommy Taylor, Jimmy White, Ralph Miller and John Meredith, who all ended up eventually following me down to the south coast. Just one season after departing Charlton, and I was on the move again!

INTERLUDE

Me and Stocksy got in the team about a similar time really. He was left-back and I was right-back, and that's how we started off. Roger Jones was in the middle of us, and we conjured up a nickname for ourselves: the Freeman, Hardy & Willis group! We had a bit of fun with that, and we were great buddies.

We used to socialise a bit when there was no game on, and we've kept in touch to this day. David being made captain didn't change the dynamic at all – at the end of the day we were two buddies, and it didn't stop us from joking and taking the piss out of each other! We had our ups and downs, being in and out of the team due to injuries, etc, but we got on great.

You've got to have a little bit of luck along the way in football, and hope it turns out positive. There was a rumour at the time that Liverpool were interested in me at one point, although all I heard about it was in the papers; it never came to anything. I had a good game here against them, and I think that's where all the talk came about.

The highlight of our time playing together was the promotion season – we had a fair few drinks after that, when we got promoted. I enjoyed myself! I also remember him in goal, fumbling around on the dead-ball line! Stocksy was a very good mate.

Terry Gulliver
Teammate at Bournemouth

FOUR

MOVING TO
THE SOUTH COAST

A new home down on the south coast, a wage increase, yet another signing-on fee, and the sun shining – what was there to not like? But there was more to it than that: for the first few years at least, Bournemouth was where I consider that I played the best football of my career.

My first impressions were pretty positive on the whole. The stadium, Dean Court, was great, and the atmosphere created by the crowd was exceptional. As the ground was effectively based in a park, the training facilities were good too. I had played in plenty of bigger stadiums, especially during my time at Charlton, but Bournemouth ticked all the boxes. For the first time in my footballing career I felt like I was wanted, and this was reflected in my performances.

Once again I found myself negotiating my contract,

although unlike last time I was firmly in the driving seat, as Bournemouth wanted me. Agents were a relatively new thing back then, but only at the highest levels. The kind of contracts I was signing didn't provide much meat on the bone with which to pay an agent from – I was being sold for a fee of £3,000, and my previous move from Charlton to Gillingham didn't involve any kind of fee. I was not quite so wet behind the ears, and I had nothing to lose by asking for what I wanted out of my contract.

As it happened, on 9th June 1966, I signed a two-year contract with Bournemouth & Boscombe Athletic Football Club (as they were then known) on a basic salary of £22 per week, in addition to £5 per appearance in the first team, plus a signing-on fee of £1,000. There were various other additions based on the number of league matches I played, which I will give you an insight into here. For instance, I got a £5 bonus fee per appearance if I played 23 matches and the team was in first position in the league, £4 if second, and £3 if third. If I completed 46 league appearances then I got a £20 bonus, and the same if we won the league, dropping to £16 for second and £9 for third.

If we reached the quarter finals of the FA Cup then all the players received a share of £720, and if we reached the quarter finals of the Football League Cup then we got a share of £600. There was also a long-service payment if you stayed with the club for five years, which I achieved, as I stayed there for six years. There was a nice additional bonus of £3 for every appearance made in the first team, and £2 for appearing in the reserves. At the end of my initial contract, I signed a new and better one – by the time I left I was on £30 per week.

As well as being the time of my signing for Bournemouth, this was of course the summer that England won the World Cup. As you would expect, this created a good feeling among the football community, as it was almost like the England team were representing us as professional players. This was especially the case for myself, having played against some of the players in the England team at various points: Roger Hunt (Liverpool), Alan Ball (Blackpool), George Cohen (Fulham), Geoff Hurst, Martin Peters and Bobby Moore (West Ham), Jack Charlton (Leeds), and my personal favourite, as I mirrored his playing position at the time, Ray Wilson of Everton. I did my best to emulate his style of play – in my opinion he is one of the best full-backs in the history of the game. He was basically a defender who could play a bit as well: very seldom beaten by the opposing winger, quick and constructive with his play, very neat and tidy, and definitely an underrated member of the World Cup team.

-

Having Freddie Cox as manager was great for me. Even though we had only worked together for just the one season at Gillingham, I knew his style very well, and he knew mine, not only as a player, but as a person. This helped enormously during my settling-in period at Bournemouth. Initially there was a bit of a tension among the existing squad due to Cox bringing so many players with him from Gillingham, but this soon settled down as the new arrivals proved their worth.

Cox's style of management did change slightly, as he seemed more relaxed at Bournemouth. Whether he was under more pressure at Gillingham to get results I don't know, but the directors of the club seemed more involved there. Conversely, their counterparts at Bournemouth came across as more at ease with letting him get on with the business of management and getting the best from the team.

I was helped by the team around me, with Cox dipping his hand into the transfer market. As well as yours truly, that summer he also signed Terry Gulliver from Weymouth, Ralph Norton from Reading and Ken Pound from Swansea. Ronnie Bolton also arrived towards the end of season from Ipswich Town, having previously played at the club from 1958 to 1965. He was a classy player, but the Third Division was a bit quick and robust for him. I think he would have been more effective playing at a higher level, but he never got the chance to prove it. He left in 1968 and moved to South Africa.

Freddie wasn't afraid to change things around. Long-serving goalkeeper David Best, having played in the first match of the 1966/67 season (a 1-1 draw away at Oxford), was dropped for the next game at home to Oldham Athletic. He was replaced by his understudy, Roger Jones. The reason for this soon became clear: the very next week, Best signed for the Latics for £15,000 – a fee questioned by many, as he was highly rated at the club, an outlook that seemed to be vindicated when he later established himself in the First Division with Ipswich.

After an opening-day draw at Oxford, followed by consecutive victories against Oldham, Scunthorpe and Brighton (with fellow new signing Tommy Taylor putting away a hat-trick), we were top of the table.

However, despite the early promise the team showed (winning eight and drawing two from the first ten games), the season was ultimately a disappointing one. Our initial winning streak was brought to an end by a 2-0 reverse at home to Workington (who would finish bottom of the table). With goals proving hard to come by (we scored just 39 in 46 games), form faltered, and we finished the season in 20th – just two points above the relegation zone, with safety not assured until April. The lack of goals was difficult to understand – we were aware of the problem, we just couldn't arrest the decline.

Defensively we were organised and sound, even with the two full-backs, Terry Gulliver and myself, both being very attack-minded and adept at providing crosses for the goalscoring forwards, Eddie Rowles, Ken Pound and Keith East, with John Hold in reserve, but it just didn't click. On a personal level it was a decent season for me, playing every game bar the last three due to a minor knee ligament injury that curtailed my season.

-

The 1967/68 season started in much the same fashion as the year before, with home victories against Bristol Rovers, Oxford and Scunthorpe bookending a 1-1 draw at Barrow. However, inconsistency and trouble on the goalscoring front saw us fall away, ultimately finishing in 13th. It wasn't all gloom though: I got the first of my two goals in a Bournemouth shirt, putting one away in a 4-1 home victory over Southport! I think the team was starting to gel following the influx of new players over the previous couple of seasons. As we saw in the following year, things were only going to get better. In the meantime, the highlight of the season – and possibly of my Cherries career – was my renewed acquaintance with Liverpool, courtesy of the FA Cup.

In what turned out to be a fairly middling league season, the FA Cup was a welcome distraction from the normal grind of league matches, especially if the club landed a top team in the draw. Back then, the FA Cup was definitely a highlight of the season, and players certainly upped their game against bigger clubs. Following a 2-0 home victory over Northampton Town courtesy of goals from Ronnie Bolton and John Hold, and a 3-1 win at non-league Walthamstow Avenue (thanks to two from Ken Pound and one from Jimmy White), the magic of the FA Cup brought Dean Court – and the town – to life. On 27th January 1968, a crowd of 24,388 (I still can't believe that they managed to fit that many into the old Dean Court) turned up to see us take on one of football's giants.

It wasn't a number that the club was used to: commentator Kenneth Wolstenholme had to climb a ladder in order to access the TV gantry on top of the stand so he could commentate for Match Of The Day. Indeed, such was the level of demand that the club hierarchy decreed that supporters had to have attended one of two home matches in order to be eligible for a match ticket. One of these games happened to be the penultimate home match before the tie: home to Bury. 10,387 fans saw us run out 1-0 winners, with Keith East bagging the winner. It was bitterly cold and the rain didn't stop, but the fans who attended were subsequently able to attend the Liverpool game, witnessing the following teams line up:

Bournemouth - Jones, Gulliver, Naylor, J White, Stocks, Bumstead, Bolton, K White, Rowles, East, Pound. Sub: Hold

Liverpool - Lawrence, Lawler, Smith, Yeats, Byrne, Strong, Hughes, Callaghan, Hunt, St.John, Thompson. Sub: Hateley.

Just five years after my debut at Anfield in a Charlton shirt, I was facing them again, with some familiar faces among their line-up: Emlyn Hughes, Roger Hunt, Ian Callaghan and Ian St John. I knew what we were up against and conveyed this to my teammates when I was asked to do the pre-match team talk by the manager. This was more nerve-racking than the match itself, but having been there and done it, Freddie Cox thought a bit of motivation from me pre-match would help the cause, so I did it, and actually enjoyed it – whether it helped or not I'm not sure. There were still some very white faces in the dressing room, with some regular trips to the toilet by certain players.

In the event, we excelled ourselves. Despite two whole divisions separating the sides, we arguably had the better of the chances, spending most of the 90 minutes hammering away at the Liverpool goal, but enjoyed little reward for our efforts. Keith East had what looked like a perfectly good goal disallowed in the 42nd minute, and Liverpool rode out their luck to hang on grimly to a goalless draw. The post-match Bill Shankly quip that Liverpool were giving us a chance to make money in a replay came from a man who knew that his team had been lucky to escape defeat. Interestingly, the replay took place three days later – a bit different to nowadays – plus of course we had to get up to Liverpool. Conveniently, we were able to fly from Bournemouth Airport and straight back by plane after the game – fairly unusual back in the day, but quite common nowadays, so I'm told!

-

The following Tuesday, at 7.30pm on 30th January 1968, under the lights at Anfield, we began where we had left off, this time in front of a crowd of 54,075. When asked what I remember in particular from that evening, the thoughts that come to mind are firstly arriving at the ground in the coach, again with a certain amount of hostility from the home supporters around the entrance. Sitting in the dressing room prior to the start, there was a deathly silence from everyone and nerves started to kick in.

When we went out to look at the pitch, the floodlights were only partially on. The supporters in the ground whistled, creating a very frightening atmosphere that took me back to my Charlton debut at Anfield, especially in the half light – it certainly got the heart rate up! Back in the dressing room, we all just sat there looking at each other, almost like we were in shock. We quickly realised that we needed to get out of this mood: we had a game to play, and a few words from the management team and the senior players put us back on track.

I was trying to stay positive. I had played here before, and it was just another game, but tensions were high. To beat Liverpool in the FA Cup and progress to the next round would be great for the club. We had a basic plan of how to play the game, which amounted to nullifying the two wingers, Thompson and Callaghan – both England internationals who normally provided the crosses for Roger Hunt and Tony Hateley. Hateley in particular was superb in the air – certainly one of the best headers of the ball at this time.

In practice, nullifying a team full of internationals proved to be easier said than done, as Liverpool regularly bought all their giants up for corners. When I say giants, I mean it – standing in front of me at the near post were Hateley, Hunt, Ron Yeats and Chris Lawler, four of the best headers of the ball in the game, with Callaghan taking the corner. Roger Jones, our keeper, was shouting at me to mark one of them, but thanks to the deafening noise from the Kop end, all I could see was his lips moving. It was incredible to experience when you consider that at the time our crowds at Dean Court were around five to six thousand – quite a contrast!

In the game itself, once again we gave Liverpool a terrific run for their money – for the first 30 minutes. The deadlock was broken when Hateley scored for Liverpool with a powerful header, and despite the setback of further goals from Thompson, Hunt and Lawler, an own goal by Emlyn Hughes was scant reward for what in actuality was a fine fighting display. We were beaten, but never out of it – not as the 4-1 scoreline suggested. On reflection it was a fantastic occasion, despite the result. Having made my league debut for Charlton back in 1961 at Liverpool, to play at Anfield again brought back great memories in what was an emotional but enjoyable evening for me.

Being on the same pitch at the same time as the likes of Roger Hunt and Emlyn Hughes was an experience too. While I didn't come up against them too much in the game itself, their physicality and work ethic stood out. Hughes especially was incredible – he was my all-time hero in any case, and it was a privilege to play against him.

The consolation – at least financially speaking – for the club was that Bournemouth would take home £5,000, their share of the cash paid by the capacity crowd. The players, however, were not rewarded so well. When we picked up our wages the following week we had an extra 10 shillings in our pay packets – not much of a bonus considering there were 24,000 at Dean Court in the first match and just over 54,000 at Anfield for the replay. Almost 80,000 people watched the two games, and we got an extra 50 pence each. For finishing all square at home against Liverpool, bonuses in the league at that time were £5 for a win and £2.50 for a draw. Regardless, as we flew back to Eastleigh after the match, where we enjoyed our chicken sandwiches, we reflected on the incredible footballing experience – plus we were all allowed a beer or two on the flight, which the club paid for.

Having played in every game that season for the first time in my career, I repeated the same feat in the following year, when we finished fourth (let down by a poor finish to the season that saw us score just eight goals in the final fourteen games). There was quite clearly a problem that I believe stemmed from the lack of creativity on the part of the midfield, which resulted in poor service for the goalscorers, and thus a lack of goals. I know I'm stating the obvious, but it's basically true. Defensively we were very sound, conceding only 36 goals in 46 matches. We had a decent enough side, with myself, Terry Gulliver, Roy Gater and Ralph Miller at the back, Roger Jones behind us and the likes of Ronnie Bolton and Ray Bumstead further forward. At their best, Freddie Cox sides were very solid defensively, and we certainly fit the bill in this regard.

Our final points tally was 51 – ten points lower than third-placed Luton, and thirteen points short of Third Division winners Watford, who we lost to both home and away. There were few positives in the FA Cup either: non-league Bury managed a 0-0 draw at home in the first round, before being beaten 3-0 in the replay at Dean Court. Bristol Rovers were then faced in round two, with a disappointing goalless draw at home being followed by a 0-1 defeat in the replay at Rovers. The League Cup was a damp squib too, finishing in the first round with a 6-1 thrashing against Southend. Truthfully, in finishing fourth, it felt like we were playing above ourselves. We simply didn't have enough about ourselves going forward.

To be fair to Cox, he tried to rectify that the following season by boosting our attacking options: Trevor Hartley arrived from West Ham, my old teammate John Meredith was picked up from Gillingham, and a lad called Ted MacDougall signed from York. Despite these reinforcements, things got worse the following season, as we picked up from where we left off form-wise. After winning just two of the first six games, we were in trouble from the get-go.

There was one bright spark, however. After holding First Division Sheffield Wednesday to a 1-1 draw at Hillsborough, we beat them 1-0 in the replay courtesy of a strike from John Hold. Victories against First Division clubs naturally attract a fair bit of attention, and this is correctly regarded as a shining light in an otherwise disastrous season. It was no fluke; we were the best team over the 90 minutes, and won the replay deservedly. For my part, my memories of the occasion centre more around the ground than the game itself. It may be hard for today's supporters to appreciate just how big Sheffield Wednesday were back then. Hillsborough was one of the biggest grounds around, and in terms of atmosphere it stands alongside Anfield and Elland Road as the best I've experienced during my playing career.

With these two games sandwiching a 5-1 away win over Tranmere (John Hold putting away a hat-trick), it looked like our luck was turning. However, it wasn't to be the case, as we spent the following 12 games winless (including crashing out of the League Cup after a 2-0 reverse at Leicester). We were in trouble. Even then, however, we looked capable of recovering. The slump was arrested by a 1-0 win against Stockport, followed by further victories against Gillingham, Doncaster and Plymouth, along with draws against Torquay, Tranmere and Brighton.

But inevitably, things fell apart once more. After a hat-trick of defeats against Rotherham, Reading and Halifax, our lack of luck was characterised in bizarre fashion away at Bradford City in January 1970. Our goalkeeper Ron Tilsed (Roger Jones had been sold to Blackburn Rovers by this point for just £30,000, a decision we would come to regret) got injured and came off at half time.

Part of the reason for our eventual relegation was our failure to adequately replace Jones. We could all see how good he was, even though he was very no-frills; he would just quietly go about his work, making saves that were beyond words. In those days, there was far less protection for keepers, who would regularly come under assault from giant forwards, but he would effortlessly deal with the numerous balls pumped into the box. Tilsed wasn't of the same standard. Not that he knew it; a young lad, he was full of himself. Nothing wrong with that if you can back it up, but he didn't. The dressing room's a small place, and if you keep talking yourself up while not producing the goods, they'll home in on you.

In those days we didn't have a substitute goalkeeper on the bench, so in the changing room Cox announced/ asked, "Tilsed is injured, who's going in goal for the second half?" Immediately, ten heads looked down at the floor. Bradford City away, 2-0 down on a cold January day – unsurprisingly there were no takers. He looked around.

"Come on," he said, "One of you needs to volunteer." Still no response. "Right," he said, "Stocksy, you play cricket, you can play in goal."

What? "I've never played in goal, and what has being able to play cricket got to do with anything?"

"If you play cricket then surely you can catch. You are going in goal, end of."

That was that. I put the goalkeeper jersey on (inadvertently leaving the gloves in the changing room, which had to be retrieved by one of the subs), and out we went for the second half. Bradford soon caught on that the new goalkeeper was the guy who was playing left-back in the first half, at which point the abuse began.

The first corner was a nightmare – where was I supposed to stand? The ball came in and I tried to punch it clear, which I just about succeeded in doing. I was almost shaking with fear, having never experienced anything in a football match like this. My next test was a penalty – what had I done to deserve this? Needless to say, they scored. The final result was 8-1 to Bradford. I resolved never to criticise a goalkeeper again. For Tilsed, that was his last match in a Bournemouth shirt. Youngster Kieron Baker ended up playing the majority of the rest of the season in goal. He went on to have a great career at Bournemouth, playing over 200 games, but he wasn't at Jones's level.

Consistency eluded us. Three wins and a draw were followed by just four points from the following eight matches. Despite going into the final game of the season with three victories from the previous five games, and a 20-goal contribution from Ted, the damage had been done.

While Ted is correctly regarded as a legend now, he had a bit of a slow start, scoring just three in his first 12 games. Part of the problem was how we were playing him – with the ball played into his feet in the box, he was lethal. Any further back just wasn't his game. We eventually cottoned on and adjusted our game accordingly, but it was too late to salvage the season.

After gaining a 0-0 draw in our final match of the season away at my old club Gillingham, leaving us three points ahead of them, we thought we might be safe, since their final match was away at league leaders Leyton Orient, and we couldn't see them picking up a result. Alas, football eluded predictability once more, as the Gills produced a shock by winning at Brisbane Road, and in doing so confined us to the drop on goal difference, with us finishing fourth from bottom and getting relegated along with Stockport, Barrow and Southport. Things were about to change – both for me and the club – in a big way.

INTERLUDE

Having signed for Bournemouth from York, up until that point I had always been based up north, so I loved how sunny it was. The weather was so warm that we couldn't train one day, so we went to the beach and I thought, "Wow, this is fantastic!" When I first saw David, he was with Terry Gulliver, and I couldn't believe how bronzed and tanned they were!

On the pitch, David was a solid defender – he was old school. If you remember, the story goes that when they signed me, they had just missed out on promotion, and they got these players – including myself – and we were expected to be going towards the top of the league. We had this really good back four, with Stocks, Terry, Ralph Miller and Jimmy White, and Roger Jones in goal. So we had a really good back five, and we were expected to do great things, but it didn't turn out that way, unfortunately.

My recollections of Stocksy was that he was different to other footballers, and I mean that in a nice way. My impression was that it wasn't the be-all and end-all for him.

It wasn't that he was this footballer who was playing because there was nothing else in life for him. I never thought Dave was like that; I always thought there was a little bit more in his locker, he was a bit more intellectual with regards to his future and his life.

The game that sticks in the mind the most when it comes to David was that defeat at Bradford when he had to go in goal. I don't remember his reaction, but I remember the goalkeeper. He was a young lad, 18 or 19, a jack the lad, and he didn't blame himself for one goal; it was nothing to do with him! I remember Stocksy went in goal. I can't quite remember – it's probably something you'd want to forget!

I liked David, and I liked what he brought to the club, and what he was as a player. He was a good pro, and appeared to me to have other things on his agenda, and other things he could accomplish, and football was just part of something he was going to do to get where he wanted to go. He was a bright kid that saw an opportunity, and was enjoying his time as a footballer, but it wasn't what he was [always] going to do.

Ted MacDougall
Teammate at Bournemouth

FIVE

STRAIGHT BACK UP

Although I felt that Freddie Cox's management style was ahead of his time back at Gillingham and certainly at the beginning of his tenure at Bournemouth, the game had moved on since then. It was more fluid and fast-moving, and unfortunately Freddie was too stuck in his ways. The club needed new initiatives if it was going to crawl back up the leagues. Subsequently, Freddie was sacked as manager. There was little in the way of fanfare; the new chairman simply walked into the changing room and said, "The manager's going," and that was it.

The new chairman in question was lifelong fan Harold Walker. While very public about his plans for the club, he had very little contact with the players, and came across to me as quiet, shy and private. He initially offered the job to Cyril Lea of Ipswich, but he took too long to make up his mind, so Walker turned to John Bond, formerly of West Ham and Torquay.

Bond didn't come alone; he brought with him Ken Brown, one of his old West Ham playing colleagues, as coach, in addition to Reg Tyrell as assistant manager. There was a completely different atmosphere with Bond in charge – he was a much younger manager, and training became more competitive and ball-based, with a set way of playing, especially for the forwards. Everyone had a clearly defined job to do, and I enjoyed training more, especially with the higher standard of players being brought to the club. Notable among the new arrivals were winger Tony Scott from York City, and Keith Miller, both former teammates of Bond's at West Ham.

Ken Brown was very much the good cop to John's bad. Where Bond was definitely not averse to losing his temper in the dressing room, calling people useless and threatening to drop them – which didn't particularly bother me, although some of the younger lads might have been affected – Ken would be quick to follow up with kinder words: "He didn't really mean what he said; he just gets carried away."

Although the atmosphere changed with the arrival of a new management team, in my opinion it wasn't as unsettling as you might imagine. We had some idea of their management style, but to be honest it was like a breath of fresh air to have some new ideas, routines and enthusiasm. I know some players didn't like change – and indeed, they were the ones to be moved on – but from my perspective I was a hard worker, and always keen to get better results, so was open to new ideas. His approach to coaching adopted the Coverdale organisation's 'positive play as a result of positive thinking training' scheme.

As to what that entailed – well, I wish I could tell you! Funnily enough, at the 50th anniversary celebration of the promotion season that took place at Dean Court in 2021, Jimmy Glass, who was compering the evening, asked us what about his approach was so different to what was in place before. None of us could provide an answer! As we later discovered, a lot of it seemed to revolve around signing players he had worked with previously who he knew and trusted.

-

My relationship with Bond was at times a difficult one, even though it started on a positive footing when he made me captain. He was intrigued by the fact that I had been taking my coaching certificates – unusual for someone at my age – and since I'd been there for a few years by that point, he thought I'd be best placed to show some of the new arrivals the ropes. So far, so good.

However, this didn't last. As time went by, it became very clear that he wanted his own players, especially any that he had worked with previously at West Ham and Torquay. This was to a certain extent understandable: recruiting players he knew and trusted. Out went the old-style training methods, and in came a modern approach that even included a new continental-looking strip. The predominantly red shirt was out, and red and black stripes were in. We may have been facing life in the Fourth Division for the 1970/71 season, but we approached it with a great air of optimism and style.

Initially, this good feeling seemed misplaced, as an opening-day defeat at Aldershot dampened spirits. It was very much a case of 'Welcome to the Fourth Division'. Aldershot isn't the most hospitable of away venues at the best of times, and that reception extended to the players. It was the first time I can recall that their right winger was kicking lumps out of me. You don't do that; it's supposed to be the other way around!

Thankfully, this turned out to be a case of teething troubles rather than a sign of things to come, as we won the next seven league matches, and MacDougall – who Bond considered getting rid of at one stage – started finding the net. Initially, Bond had had doubts about Ted's ability, as he had expected him to be a contributor to the setting up of goals, but his role became clearer with the inclusion of Phil Boyer as a second striker who took on the role of setting up play. Ted was there to just tap it home – or more likely, rocket the ball into the back of the net with his head or feet! In the sixth of those games, Colchester felt the force of 'Super Mac' as he scored all four goals in a 4-1 win. It became a running theme: feed Ted, and he would score.

Phil was Ted's godsend. Ted was actually quite shy, but we sat next to each other in the changing rooms, so we spoke a lot, and got on well. Myself and Gully would say to him, "Ted, you score goals for fun, we don't want you coming short to get the ball; we want you in the 18-yard box." He said, "That's exactly what I want." The answer to making things easier for him was signing Phil, his old teammate at York. We had played against him a few times, so we were familiar with him, and it was well received when Bond signed him.

However, I wasn't faring so well. Part of this was due to me and Bond not really mixing. Ironically, since it was originally a reason for him to assign me the captaincy, I think he felt threatened by the fact that I had my coaching badges (he needn't have been – management didn't interest me in the slightest at that point!). Added to this, I was forced to adapt my playing style to what Bond wanted from me. While before I was very much an overlapping full-back who would ping crosses into Ted for him to put away, Bond instructed me to sit back and concentrate on defending. Instead, I was instructed to pass it on to the left winger in front of me, Tony Scott – or to Phil Boyer – and let them provide the assists.

The logic wasn't hard to see; Scotty was a better crosser of the ball than me. But I enjoyed getting forward, and while I obeyed instructions to concentrate on my defensive duties, it did take the fun out of playing a bit. Not that I had a choice; if I didn't agree then I would be out of the team, simple as that. It was a far cry from my time at Gillingham as an overlapping full-back, switching positions with John Meredith. My style of play had changed instantly, which took some getting used to. On top of that, my game became much more physically demanding. With my attacking duties reduced to almost nothing, I'd come off at the end of games battered and bruised. I wasn't getting any younger either, which made the experience even more difficult.

As it turned out, the sense I got that Bond didn't fancy

me all that much as a player wasn't without foundation. After a 4-2 defeat at Chester, I was dropped from the line-up. It wasn't discussed beforehand, and no reason was given; the first I heard about it was the same time as everyone else: when the team sheet was pinned up in the dressing room for the following game, against Lincoln. I wasn't even named on the bench. I did notice in Neil Vacher's excellent book, *Goal Along With The Cherries*, that Bond said he'd discussed the reasons for the changes with me. That's certainly news to me!

In any case, I was out of the team. Tony Powell moved across to left-back, and Keith Miller took the captaincy. No hard feelings there – when you've played as much as I have, you understand that it's just a fact of life. You just have to get on with things. Being out of the team meant that I missed a number of the season's highlights, such as Ted hitting the national press in November with a six-goal haul in an 8-1 FA Cup win against Oxford City. The cobwebs that had settled around the club over the years were being blown away, as our almost cavalier approach to matches was gaining the required results, and we were firm promotion contenders.

While going from captain and former player of the year to being out of the picture wasn't a nice experience, I remained supportive of the team, going to games and turning out for the reserves (our home games were played at Fernheath in West Howe – very much a far cry from some of the stadiums I had played in previously!).

Bond further strengthened the side by bringing in Mel Machin from Gillingham around halfway through the season at full-back – displacing my mate Terry Gulliver who, unlike me, never found his way back in as a regular starter – which built a strong foundation in defence. Mel was a different player to me; not particularly physical, but good on the ball. His first touch was excellent, and he had a wide range of passing. His tackling was probably his weakest point, but he had a good turn of pace, which got him out of trouble on the odd occasion. It came as no surprise that he later went into management, as he came across as a very thoughtful and interesting character. Out of all the new signings, Phil Boyer was the one who made the most difference, supplying the ammunition for MacDougall to devastating effect. Crowds were virtually doubled as scorelines of 4-1 and 4-2 became commonplace. Dean Court was the place to be.

Eventually, my exile from the first team came to an end when I was reinstated for the 1-0 defeat at Grimsby. I found out the same way as I had about being dropped: by seeing the team sheet pinned to the dressing room door. Arthur Cunliffe, the trainer, would walk into the dressing room on the Friday, announce "Runners and riders", pin the sheet to the door, and that was it. There was no real discussion, at least not with me.

Thankfully, the Grimsby game – the third of a rare winless patch in that season – proved to be an outlier. After a 2-1 win on the road at Barrow and a draw against Scunthorpe (who had a young Kevin Keegan in their line-up – not that I remember him standing out, although my friend Steve Webb recalls him having a decent game), we just couldn't seem to stop scoring. The remainder of

January saw three consecutive home victories (5-0 against Oldham, 4-2 against Northampton and 4-1 against Exeter) capped off by a 3-3 stalemate at Crewe.

Crewe is another game that stands out due to the presence of a certain Stan Bowles. He was yet to reach the career heights he'd subsequently hit, but he was still a lively presence, assisting for their second and scoring one himself for their third, the equaliser. Unsurprisingly, a lot of their play went through him, which he tended to direct round the pitch. He didn't stay on my side for long though – after two or three heavy tackles, he cleared off to the other wing. It was a memorable game – although the less said about the penalty I gave away, the better! We were going into games fully expecting to win, and for good reason. When you had someone like Ted in your team, you knew that it was just a matter of providing him with chances. As long as the defence then did their jobs, the game was as good as won.

The crunch game came on 6th February 1971 when Bournemouth – then in second place – took on top-of-the-table Notts County. The crowd of 15,431 saw a 1-1 draw – a fantastic attendance for the Fourth Division. Notts County were our rivals by default, and it was a tasty affair. I myself only lasted 16 minutes, requiring medical attention in the form of stitches to my head after clashing with their winger. While Notts County had a robust approach – Bond was pretty scathing about their tactics, saying, "I would rather pack in the game than allow my team to play this way" – they were worthy eventual league champions. They had some excellent players: Brian Stubbs was a mainstay of the team, staying with them throughout their subsequent rise to the First Division, and Tony Hateley up front was always a menace. Having played against me in the FA Cup replay at Liverpool a few years back, he had returned to his home-town club (although not before short-lived stints at Coventry and Birmingham), but still knew where the goal was. Charlie Crickmore also stands out. The makeweight in my move to Bournemouth from Gillingham (although he claims it was the other way around!), we always got on well. The main dangerman, however, was Don Massey, who funnily enough nearly ended up at Bournemouth at one point. We gave Keith Miller the task of marking him – we didn't lose, so we had some small success in that regard!

Saying that, the result pretty much ended our chances of pipping County for the title. Ultimately, we weren't quite consistent enough to claim the top spot. We followed up Notts County with a 3-2 victory over Northampton, only to go down 1-0 at home to Southport. Further victories against Lincoln and Chester were accompanied by defeats to Workington and Hartlepool, along with a goalless draw at home to Barrow.

Going into the final run-in, MacDougall could not stop scoring, and promotion was looking all the more likely. Out of the remaining 10 games, Ted scored ten to go along with them. A 1-0 win at home to Darlington was followed by 1-1 draws against Stockport and Newport (Ted the sole scorer). We battered Southend 4-0 at home, then drew 0-0 away at Exeter. This was followed up by 2-0 and 1-0 victories against Cambridge and Brentford respectively, and then a 1-1 tie at Colchester.

Ultimately, promotion was sealed when Chester lost at Exeter, so without us kicking a ball (we had drawn 1-1 at Colchester the night before, Ted again the scorer) we were promoted at the first attempt; Notts County were already champions at that point. Was it an anti-climax? Not really, no. We just wanted promotion, and didn't care how we got it. In our minds, we never should have been in that position in the first place, so it was the least that we deserved.

All that was left was the question of whether Ted could find the net for the 50th time. Having put one away in our 3-1 reverse at Peterborough (we'd probably taken our foot off the pedal a bit at that point), he went into the final game on 1st May 1971 against his old club, York, on 47 goals, and finished on 49 as we beat York 4-0, with Boyer and Tony Scott grabbing one apiece. He came agonisingly close to the half century when a cross from Keith Miller hit the inside of his heel – it just wasn't to be! Not that Ted seemed too fazed – he was fairly nonchalant about the 50-goal target. He was not really driven by the numbers; he was only interested in scoring goals, which he was incredibly good at.

As the referee blew the final whistle, the crowd invaded the pitch to celebrate the club's first ever promotion in the club's history. These celebrations continued on an open-top bus along Ashley Road, Christchurch Road and then down Sea Road to the Neptune bar at Boscombe Pier. The roads were lined with well-wishers and supporters cheering us on. As for us, the celebrations weren't especially manic (although me and Gully went down town a fair bit!).

Ultimately, it was a case of job done. After a brief Fourth Division tour, we were back in the Third Division.

-

Ted was undoubtedly the catalyst of the team; his goal haul was staggering, although he was sometimes a difficult guy to play with because he only had one thing on his mind: scoring goals. Conversely, the likes of Boyer, John Sainty and Tony Scott were a pleasure to play alongside; Ted only really came to life when he got in front of the goal. Our game plan was to keep him out of the build-up as much as possible and make sure we got the ball in the box to him. Often today you see forwards dropping deep to receive the ball – out and out strikers are an increasingly rare breed. Not so with Ted: we did the heavy lifting for him while he stayed up the pitch.

His timing for finishing off crosses was superb – he would leave space in front of the goal, so he was on the move forwards when the cross came in, enabling him to have a running jump on the defender, which created power for his header or shot. At times he was unstoppable, being very clear that his role in the side was to score goals, which he did incredibly well. While Phil often gets the plaudits for supplying Ted, Tony Scott, who normally played on the left wing, deserves a mention for his great service for Ted. He was very much in the habit of crossing the ball very early, which enabled Ted to get the jump on his marker and finish the job off.

Other teammates during my time at the club included

Ray Bumstead, a very underrated player who immediately brings to mind all the boring words used to describe players like him: consistent, hard-working and effective. As committed a full-back as he was a winger, he worked well defensively and was a good trainer, scoring the odd goal and certainly making a few scoring chances for other players. He had a good business head, running a hairdressing business while he was playing, and was a really nice and amusing guy, with 414 league appearances (currently fourth in the all-time Bournemouth appearance stakes behind Steve Fletcher, Neil Young and Sean O'Driscoll), and 55 goals to his name.

Another personality in the squad at this time was hard-tackling defender Tony Powell. With his boxing background, he and I provided the grit in defence. He wasn't someone I would generally socialise with, but he was a very valuable member of the team, with a good attitude to the game. He was a favourite of the crowd due to his physical approach, which would liven up many a Saturday afternoon at Dean Court.

Roger Jones was the best goalkeeper I ever played with. He commanded his area well, seldom making mistakes and displaying fantastic handling in the air. He signed from Portsmouth in 1965, went on to play for England Under 23s, and moved to Blackburn Rovers in 1969. He was part of the Freeman, Hardy & Willis group – sometimes called the 'Holy Trinity' – as he, myself and my best mate Terry Gulliver were known back in the late '60s during the Freddie Cox era. We were so named as when the team for the Saturday match was pinned up on the notice board in the home dressing room on a Friday morning after training, the first three names consistently on the team sheet were Roger, Terry and me.

Interestingly, if we had lost our previous game then there would quite often be a practice match mid-week on the main pitch, with us back three playing in the reserve team against the first team. This was a psychological test from the manager to motivate us to try harder – the alternative was being dropped. However, come Friday morning we were always back on the team sheet.

Terry Gulliver, a good friend of mine, was an easy-going local player from Salisbury, signed by Freddie Cox from Weymouth at the same time as me in 1966. He should have played at a higher level – indeed, Liverpool were interested in signing him at one point. With me at left-back, 'Gully' at right-back and Roger Jones in goal, we were the backbone of the defence in the team for a number of years, with Jones making 160 league appearances, Terry 164 and me 220.

The level of professionalism within the game nowadays is far more pronounced compared to what it was back then, which you would expect. Nonetheless, allow me to outline to you a week in the life of Bournemouth & Boscombe Athletic during the late '60s and early '70s, including our nutrition and general fitness regime!

Sunday

The day off after the match on Saturday. I would head to the ground for treatment if injured, although any that was administered was fairly basic – not like today with the medically qualified physios and sport science departments. I personally would use ice on any injury after the game, although this was not advised by the club. If uninjured, I would have a hot bath in the evening in preparation for training on Monday morning, by which point hopefully the aches and pains from Saturday would have gone or eased off.

Monday

If we had a good result on Saturday then we may be given this day off as well. However, if the result was not favourable or our performance had been poor then we were served our punishment, which would include a team meeting with the manager, where a lot of straight talking took place, along with some form of punishment, which would generally involve a significant amount of running or weight training. If we got the day off, a few of us would go and play a round of golf or squash – it was a good way to keep us out of the bar!

Tuesday

Training for Tuesday was always a hard-running day, especially if there was no mid-week game. The first-team squad – about 15 or so players – would do sessions of running, either around the pitch or behind the stand at the ground on the tarmac. We would do shuttle runs of about 50 yards back and forth, then the running around the pitch would be to instructions of 2-4-6-8, which meant that as a group we would run two laps around the pitch on the gravel, followed by four half laps and then six side laps (ie, from one end to the other), and finally eight quarter laps. These would all be done on a sprint basis in teams of five. John Bond and Ken Brown tended to take these sessions, and were very hands-on with them, which isn't always the case today, depending on the coaching setup. John Kirk took the reserves, while Trevor Hartley combined his playing duties with taking charge of the youth team.

The number of sessions depended on how well we were coping with them, or if it was felt that we weren't trying hard enough, at which point the number would increase. Most of these running-day training sessions were hosted by Michael Wheeler. A Bronze medal winner in the 4 x 400 metres relay at the 1956 Olympic Games in Melbourne, at this point he was also a sports teacher at Castle Court School in Corfe Mullen. One of his drills had one player trying to sprint while the other held a rope or long band around him to create resistance.

After the running, we would move on to some ball work, which only lasted about ten minutes or so, and would be followed by a seven- or eight-a-side match. This would take place on the tarmac behind the stand, and could get quite aggressive, especially if we played as teams of English players against the rest of the UK, or first team against the reserves and juniors. It tended to be those on the fringes of the team who got the most feisty, but the regular starters were quite capable of looking after themselves.

Wednesday

Probably a practice match on the main pitch against

Proof of my goalscoring days as a schoolboy! (Evening Standard)

South London lead through Stocks

Evening Standard Football Reporter

A goal by left-half Stocks after 25 minutes gave South London Boys an interval lead in their Corinthian Shield fourth round tie against East Ham Boys here at Flanders Field, East Ham, today.

East Ham opened well with some clever approach work but after 25 minutes a 15-yard lob from left-half STOCKS beat East London's goalkeeper Watkins.

Slater, in South London's goal, ended many promising East Ham raids. Other good moves were spoilt by poor finishing.

South London came into the game in the later stages of the half and only good work by the home defence prevented them increasing their lead.

Half-time: East Ham 0, South London 1.

BOYS' RESULTS

London Schools' Charity Cup.—
Ilford 2, East London 1.

London Schools team

London Schools team to play Manchester in an inter-city match at Manchester on Wednesday (7.30) is :—

R Allen (NW Middlesex); T More (Heston), D Stocks (Sth London); E Presland (East Ham), B Wilson (Bedford), L Picking (Tottenham); W Belger (Wood Green), R Boyce (East Ham), R Chandler (Luton), R Hunt (Colchester), M Broad (Edmonton).

STOCKS HIT TWO GOALS

SOUTH LONDON BOYS 2 CROYDON BOYS 1

Standard Football Report

Stocks scored a goal in each half to give South London Boys victory over Croydon Boys in the second round Hood Shield tie at East Dulwich today.

South London deserved more than their 2—1 victory. One of their players, Goodall, left the field with a groin injury 15 minutes from the end, but they maintained a barrage at Croydon's goal.

STOCKS put South London ahead in the fifth minute with a low shot. Goalkeeper Johnson failed to measure the curve of its flight and he was well beaten.

Half-time: South London 1, Croydon 0.

There was an exciting opening in the second half. Inside-right Nightingale cracked in a hard shot which goalkeeper Johnson did well to tip over the bar. Goodall hit the bar with the corner kick and STOCKS headed the ball home for South London's second goal.

Croydon's goal came when YARNLEY scored from a position which appeared to be offside.

Schools' Soccer

EAST HAM HIT 'LATE WINNER

EAST HAM 2 STH. LONDON 1

One goal down at half-time, East Ham fought back to qualify for the semi-final of the Corinthian Shield when they beat South London at Flanders Field to-day.

First-half honours went to South London, STOCKS scoring in the 25th minute. Their well planned approach work opened gaps in East Ham's defence.

Only some splendid saves by Watkins and good covering by Gibbens kept the visitors from going further ahead.

East Ham equalised three minutes after the restart, when BOYCE netted with a fierce drive. A minute from time PETRIPHER scored the match-winning second in a goalmouth scramble.

Late goal decides

Manchester Boys 1, London Boys 2

A goal seven minutes from time gave London Boys an unnerved victory under the Maine-road lights last night in a game which never achieved the quality expected.

Manchester took the lead in the seventh minute when right Davies and winger Creilin cut the London defence for centre forward Dean to score.

The London side were rattled for a time, but equalised through Belgar, and just when a draw seemed certain, Broad hit the winner through a ruck of defenders.

ASSOCIATION

SCOTTISH LEAGUE — Division 1: Ayr (2) 2, Queen's Park (1) 1.

European Cup.—Semi-final (first leg): Real Madrid, holders (2) 4, Vasas (Hungary) 0. Second leg in Budapest on May 15.

Lancashire Amateur Cup.—Semi-final: Chorlton 1 (Wallis), Liverpool Police 0. (At The Cliff, Broughton.)

Lancashire Combination.—Div 1: Morecambe 0, Wigan Ath. 1.

Inter-City Match.—Manchester Boys 1 (Dean), London Boys 2 (Belgar, Broad). (At Maine-road.)

Manchester Wednesday League.—Div 1: Bolton Markets 4, Manchester Fire Brigade 1. Postal Athletic 4, R.A.F. (Wilmslow) 0. Salford Police 5, Daily Express 0. Hyde-road 6, R.A.F. (Wilmslow) "A" 2. Div II: Allied Dairies 3, Queen's-road 2.

Tour Match.—Andennes (Belgium) 7, Liverpool University 1. (At Andennes.)

BOWLS

Panel games.—At Westhoughton: Cons. T. Tinker, Huddersfield (2), 41; G. Howarth, Kearsley (scr), 55. W. Molyneux, Wigan (1 and jack), 41, N. Norris, Dukinfield (scr), 19. Today: Chorley (1.0).

MERCURY SEEK A CLUB-ROOM

MERCURY F.C., formed in November, 1957, finished runners-up in their first full season last year in the West Fulham Authentic League, being awarded the Sportsmanship Cup and Secretaria's Cup.

At the beginning of the past season, Mercury entered the Invicta League Division III, determined to beat their previous season's record. But they were beaten in the Invicta Senior Lower Cup semifinal by Streatham Social (Div. II) — this being their only defeat of the season.

However they succeeded in winning the league championship, only dropping one point in 26 games and a goal average of 137 for, 34 against.

Leading goalscorers this season are Skinner 43, Robinson 24, Richardson 23, Lovell 20, and Fry 19. Albert Lovell and Alec Lambert were the only two ever-presents in the season.

Mercury are appealing for suitable premises for use as a club-room, and would be grateful if any readers can help them.

PICTURE SHOWS: Back row (left to right) — D. Stocks, D. Clarke, J. Lambert, M. Byrne, A. Lambert, A. Lovell and J. Quick. Front row (left to right) — G. Richardson, W. Robinson, S. Skinner, P. Harger, M. Fry, and C. Garvey.

(Above) Lining up with Mercury FC, the Sunday morning team I continued to play for even after signing professional terms. I'm not in kit in this photo, just in case Charlton spotted me! (Author's own collection)

(Below) Never too old for a snowball fight. (Author's own collection)

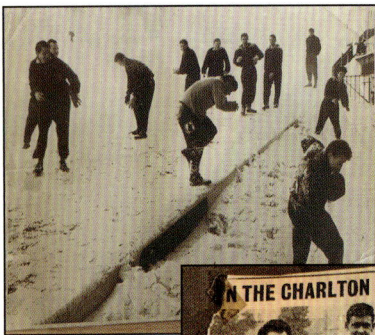

DAVID STOCKS LOOKS A CHARLTON PROSPECT

We know money is tight at The Valley, but Charlton simply must find a means of taking under their wing 18-year-old David Stocks, the finest full-back prospect we have seen at The Valley in years. Against Arsenal Colts in a Saturday match that attracted only 104 spectators young Stocks had that classy look that immediately focussed experienced eyes upon him. He is a player with a big future.

Bigger and stronger Arsenal just had the edge of the Charlton youngsters to win 2-1, yet with a little more strength and persistence at inside-forward, the home team would have won.

Fred Saunders at outside-right was another Charlton player who bore that promising look, while centre-half Albert Putnam, despite his lack of inches, looks likely to develop into a first-rate player. Kenny Bull scored Charlton's goal from an opening made by Frank Shed.

Charlton's team was: R. Avery; M. Hendy, D. Stocks; R. Harford, A. Putnam, F. Shed; F. Saunders, K. Bull, F. Randall, L. Glover, R. Campbell. Tomorrow (11 a.m.) at New Eltham, Charlton Colts play Watford.

(Above) My potential as a footballer didn't go entirely under the radar (Evening Standard)

IN THE CHARLTON JERSEY

EAGER COLTS—This was Charlton's team against Fulham in the S.E. Counties League Cup-tie at New Eltham, last Saturday. Back row (left to right): Albert Putnam, David Stocks, Ron Avery, Trevor Wales, George Cox, Barry Cordjohn. Front row: Len Glover, Kenny Bull, Michael Harrington, Pat Donovan and Brian Coombes. (" " Photo No. D.8620).

(Right) Lining up with the Colts team. (Evening Standard)

(Right) Lining up in the Charlton Squad, along side some great players including internationals such as Mike Bailey and Eddie Firmani. (Evening Standard)

Charlton's first team squad. Back row (left to right): Billy Bonds, John Sneddon, Frank Haydock, Brian Tocknell, Mike Rose, John Hewie, David Stocks, Mike Bailey, Les Glover. Front: Mike Kenning, Jack Kennedy, Roy Matthews, Keith Peacock, Brian Kinsey, Eddie Firmani. (K/1744)

AETOLIAN LEAGUE ROUND-UP

Cup Star Townsend Down To Earth

"Evening News" Reporter

FROM the excitement of an FA Cup-tie before 20,000 fans to the comparative quiet of Aetolian League soccer before a few hundred spectators, in one week. That is the outlook for Charlton's transfer-seeking full-back Don Townsend.

The dapper Townsend replaced the injured Hewie in Charlton's first team last week and did much to keep the Scunthorpe forwards at bay in a thrilling Cup tussle. Tomorrow he is named as right-back in Charlton's "A" side to travel to Gray Wanderers.

Townsend will be partnered by a young amateur, David Stocks, while at centre-half Charlton are giving a second trial to Ken Maynard, 21-year-old amateur, who a few weeks ago was with the RAF in Aden.

STOCKS TURNS PRO.

David Stocks, 19-year-old left-back who makes Charlton Reserves and formerly played for the colts, this week became a part-time professional at The Valley. Apart from football David is still continuing his studies as an articled draughtsman.

BEATEN BY BOTTOM DOGS

Charlton tried out a 19-year-old right-back, David Webster from Cambridge, in the Football Combination game with the bottom club, Brentford, at The Valley on Wednesday night. The youngster played well, but was carried off with an injury after 45 minutes. David Stocks (left-back) gave a fine display in his first game as a Charlton professional. But the forwards couldn't get goals, and Brentford won 1-0. Their goal came in the first half, after the ball had rebounded from the crossbar. Only VIP people attended, and the pitch was churned into a quagmire.

QUITE A NUMBER of Charlton fans remarked on the fine promise shown by amateur full-back David Stocks after the London Challenge Cup-tie with Chelsea at The Valley on Monday last week. David, a draughtsman apprentice, has played for Charlton since he left school, and shows steady improvement. He was in the Surrey Schools' XI when Charlton first spotted him.

STOCKS MAKES HIS LEAGUE DEBUT

Charlton lost 2-0 at Preston on Saturday, and after a week-end stay at Blackpool, played Liverpool, the Second Division champions, at Anfield on Monday, losing 2-1 after putting on their finest display since winning 4-1 at Luton in February.

In the Liverpool match, Charlton were forced to make defensive changes owing to Marvin Hinton suffering a severe thigh injury at Preston.

Brian Tocknell played at centre-half, with John Hewie right-half, and 19-year-old David Stocks making his League debut at left-back. The youngster played a great game.

Charlton played far better football than the champions, and took the lead through Bailey in 60 minutes, but Liverpool came back, equalised and notched the winner which seconds only remained.

MONDAY'S CUP-TIE

Next Monday (7.30) at The Den, New Cross, Charlton play Millwall for the Kent Challenge Cup.

('K.I.' Sports Editor)

DAVID STOCKS, the young Charlton full-back who made his League debut in the last match of the season at Liverpool, is now performing useful deeds in the cricket field with Harveys Sports Club. Playing for Harveys first 'XI last week-end, young David took 8 Dartford wickets at a cost of only 12 runs, and I hear he is also a very useful bat.

DAVID STOCKS, Charlton's latest professional, is an 18-year-old left back of great promise. He comes from West Dulwich and is a former Surrey and South London Schools' player. David is a part-timer with Charlton, and is an apprentice draughtsman.

(Left) A collection of cuttings kept by my parents from my early days at Charlton. I'll always be thankful to them for keeping these by. (Evening Standard)

CHARLTON ATHLETIC

David Stocks Talks On . . . . MY JOB

CHARLTON ATHLETIC F.C.

WALSALL

SATURDAY, 29th MARCH, 1963

6d OFFICIAL PROGRAMME

TOKEN No. 42 1961/62

LIVERPOOL FOOTBALL CLUB

FOOTBALL LEAGUE

LIVERPOOL v CHARLTON ATHLETIC

AT ANFIELD

MONDAY, 30th APRIL, 1962 Kick-off 7.15 p.m.

OFFICIAL PROGRAMME

PRICE THREEPENCE

My bio in a match day programme and the matchday programme from my debut match against Liverpool. (Charlton Athletic Museum)

IT'S TAMBLING THE MENACE

He races in to revive Chelsea

From HAROLD PALMER

CHARLTON, Saturday.

Two scrap goals from Bobby Tambling revived Chelsea in a hard game with Charlton here today.

(Left) Facing off Barry Bridges of Chelsea. I'm in the middle of the wall, flanked by John Hewie and Marvin Hinton. (Evening Standard)

(Below) Leapfrog! Very professional training hijinks in the snow. (Evening Standard)

Leaping Towards Wembley

Training for the Cup-tie with Cardiff City Charlton players

Charlton Out Of The Cup

BRILLIANT CHELSEA WIN WITH EASE

STRONGER in every department, Chelsea never had an anxious moment in the fourth round F.A. Cup-tie at The Valley on Wednesday, and were well worthy of their clear-cut 3—0 win over luckless Charlton.

Apart from the early injury to right-winger Mike Kenning, which rendered him ineffective for the rest of the game, Charlton had no excuses. They never matched Chelsea in chasing or tackling power and were always playing second fiddle to the smartest footballing outfit seen at The Valley this season. The crowd numbered 37,522, the best at Charlton since the fourth round Cup-tie with Everton in January, 1959, when the attendance numbered 44,094.

CHARLTON'S young left-back David Stocks wins this battle in the Valley mud. He slithers into the tackle to rob Norwich right-winger Gerry Mannion, the one-time Wolves star, of the ball.

Some cuttings from my time at Gillingham, including a Charlton reunion and an encounter with Alan Ball. (Evening Standard)

Blackpool 5, Gillingham 2

GILLINGHAM are out of the Football League Cup—bulldozed out by a team completely and mercilessly superior in almost every department. Not even the most wide-eyed optimist could have expected Gillingham to overcome first division Blackpool. But, though they were not disgraced, the Gills just didn't look like even loosening the strangle-hold the Blackpool forwards had on this game.

With a swirling, irritating drizzle sweeping the pitch, no-one really looked for class football. But almost from the kick-off Blackpool settled down to the conditions, mastered the slippery turf and set about pummelling Gillingham with the skill of trained ice-skaters.

As far as the fleet-footed Blackpool forwards were concerned, this could have been a sunny afternoon instead of the cold, wet Wednesday evening it was as, oblivious of the rain and wind, they slipped straight into the top-year football exclusive to division one.

Supremely fit and confident the seaside club gave Gillingham little chance to form a pattern and, though Gillingham had to contend with a bit of shirt pulling and other infringements, they were soon the goal down when centre forward Ray Charnley streaked through to blast the home even though he was not down as he let fly straight from the inside forward Alan Ball from the wing with it, only to have it disallowed for being just off-side.

SLICK GILLINGHAM BAFFLE BRIGHTON

GILLINGHAM 3, BRIGHTON 1

GILLINGHAM look promotion material. They gained a convincing win that never looked in doubt after Two yeagrs home a cross by left-back Stocks in the third minute.

Gillingham were strong and determined in the tackle and much more mobile. Their defence rarely gave Brighton an opening, although some of the visitors' midfield play looked promising.

Centre-forward Livesey was the only forward of note in the Brighton attack. His experience and skill was always evident, yet he rarely outwitted the resolute White.

The Brighton defence could not cope with a lively Gillingham forward line, in which Gibbs was the star.

Gibbs scored the second when he powered on a back pass by Baxter and gave Powney no chance.

Gillingham had an unusual formation with two strikers up field, Freeman and Gibbs, and Backstraw and the wingers playing deep.

Stocks head saves Charlton from defeat

By MIKE GRADE

Ipswich 1, Charlton 1

CHARLTON cheated Ipswich in the dying seconds—a bullet header from centre forward Gerry Baker was headed out of the goal by Charlton left back David Stocks.

The referee waved play on, but both players later confirmed that the ball was over the line. Said Stocks: "I was standing on the line, and dived backwards to get the ball."

Baker endorsed that opinion. But it was poetic justice. For Ipswich had equalised with a harshly awarded penalty after left winger Frank Brogan had been scrappily tackled.

A third-minute goal, made for centre forward Eddie Firmani by right back John Hewie, gave Charlton an early lead.

CLUB NOTES

FRANK HAYDOCK'S return to the Charlton defence at Ipswich last Saturday undoubtedly made a big difference and coincided with a definite improvement in all departments of our side. Still short of match practice, Frank didn't cover the ground he normally does, but this was only to be expected. The great thing is that Frank's back.

Just when we were beginning to feel that Charlton had at last got a grip on the injury bugbear, along comes another string of casualties. Last Saturday wing-half Peter Hawley was assisted off with a badly bruised shin in the reserve game at The Valley. At Stevenage in a Metropolitan League game inside-right Peter Reeves suffered a severe ankle injury, and over at New Eltham in the morning goalkeeper Leslie Surman sustained a severe sprain of the shoulder ligaments in the South-east Counties League match with Queen's Park Rangers.

TRUE TO THE CHARLTON TRADITION

In two cases, Charlton were leading when the injuries occurred. But that is how it goes, and we are not complaining. The great thing is that our players, true to the Charlton tradition, fight even harder when beset with unexpected setbacks.

The point at Ipswich last Saturday proved the ideal morale booster. The Ipswich lads had beaten Portsmouth 7-0 in their previous home game and confidently expected to add Charlton's scalp, especially as they had a costly new recruit at right-half—Cyril Lea from Leyton Orient.

But Charlton had other ideas and so dominated play in the first half that our half-time lead should have been much greater than 1-0. However, the big contingent of Valley fans who made the journey to Ipswich had plenty to shout about and were delighted to see the Valiants shaping to far greater purpose than in recent matches.

DAVID KEPT BROADFOOT QUIET

The second half saw Ipswich fighting back with tremendous vigour and it was unfortunate that Haydock conceded the penalty from which Baxter put the home team level. But a point away from home was very satisfying after the lean period which preceded it. One of the features was the fine play of David Stocks in taming the Ipswich right-winger, Joey Broadfoot, and David's spectacular last minute dive to head the ball off his goal-line.

Roy Matthews travelled to Ipswich but finished up as twelfth man, and it is very interesting to note that Roy's standing down broke a sequence of 65 consecutive first-team appearances for the club. The team was: Wakeham; Hewie, Stocks; Bailey, Haydock, Kinsey; Kenning, Kennedy, Firmani, Edwards, Glover. In the Ipswich goal, Thorburn did well to save two terrific shots from Mike Bailey, fresh from his success in the England teams against Wales at Wembley only a few days previously. Well done, Mike.

(Above) Clearing the steeplechase hurdle during a training session. This proved to be an inappropriate activity, as Tommy Taylor (to the right of me in the photo) caught his right foot, injuring himself and missing a few games. The photo also makes me chuckle because it was intended to include all the new players. They wanted me in the middle, as I was the marquee signing! (Author's own collection)

GILLS MET CHARLTON IN PREVIEW

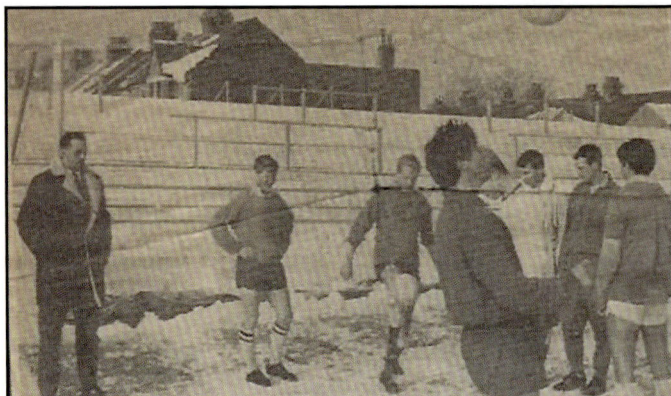

This photo perhaps demonstrates how much my face didn't fit with the new manager. I'm the only one in tracksuit trousers training in the snow – the rest of the lads were all tough northerners, while I was known as the soft southerner (but not on the pitch!). (Author's own collection)

(Left) Leading out the Cherries. (Copyright unknown)

(Below) One of my many signature left footed tackles. How I was known as a cultured left-back I will never know! (Copyright unknown)

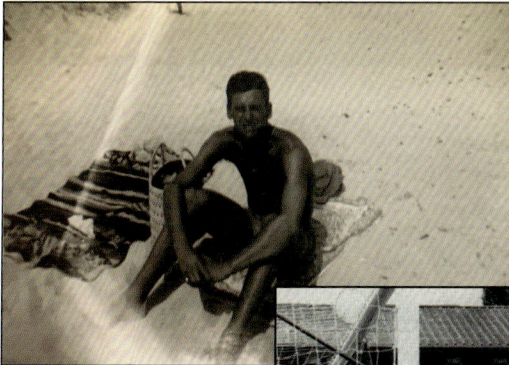

(Above) A nod to Ted MacDougall – this is how we managed to get our all-year-round tans! (Author's own collection)

(Right) Holding the line during a home win against Rotherham. (AFC Bournemouth)

(Left) Contesting the all-important coin toss with West Ham's Billy Bonds ahead of a 1970 pre-season friendly. (Bournemouth Daily Echo)

Star Stocks mixes it

BOURN'M'TH 2, OXFORD U. 1

DAVID STOCKS, cleverly mixing attack with what should have been a defensive role, was one of the main reasons for Bournemouth's win.

Stocks carved out plenty of openings and would have had even more success if there had been extra punch in the middle.

Bournemouth, becoming the early pace-makers in the Third Division, must make more of their chances if they are to keep it going.

Teenager Hold, one forward with the right idea, scored the opening goal from Kevin White's cross.

Instead of consolidating Bournemouth relaxed a little, and Oxford grabbed a quick equaliser, through Graham Atkinson.

Oxford did well enough to stay level, and Bournemouth manager Freddie Cox said that their build-up was superior to his own team's.

For all that, Oxford did not look good in defence, and Bournemouth went in front again with a header by Pound, in-off the same post as the Oxford goal.

BOURNEMOUTH: Jones 6; Gulliver 5, White (J) 6, Naylor 7, *STOCKS 9; Gater 7, Hall 7; White (K) 8, Pound 6, Hold 6, Burnstead 6.

OXFORD: Sherratt 6; Beavon 6, Clarke 7, Kyle 5, Shuker 6; Atkinson (R) 5, Jones 6; Skeen 6, Bullock 6, *ATKINSON (G) 8, Thornley 7.

Referee: L. Callaghan (Mer. Tydfil) 7.

Some cuttings from my time at Bournemouth. (Bournemouth Daily Echo)

Toning up—sauna style

What's this then—a Boscombe victory celebration? No, just a sauna bath training session with the hope that a victory might be the result. Manager Freddie Cox is putting his players through some rigorous training in the next three weeks but started it off with some toning up with a difference at the Pier Approach Bath in Bournemouth.

In the picture below, trainer John Kirk makes a note of Ray Bumstead's statistics—5ft. 8in. and 10st. 13b.—while his colleagues smile for our cameraman, Roland Evans.

From the left there is club captain Jimmy White, grinning cheekily from behind some Swedish wood—Tony Priscott, Rodney Adams (half-hidden), David Stocks, Terry Gulliver and Chris Weller.

In the picture left, the six players manage to raise a smile while they sweat away those unwanted pounds. At the back Ken Pound, Joe Ashworth, Roger Jones and Tom McKechnie while Rod Taylor and Roy Gater are the players in the front.

Sauna session for the Cherries

Cox heroes land £5,000 gate prize

By NORMAN GILLER: Liverpool 4 Bournemouth 1

(F.A. Cup, third round replay)

THE highly valued head of **Tony Hateley** finally broke Bournemouth's brave hearts at Anfield last night.

Bournemouth had silenced even the Kop choir as they held the Liverpool attack in a defensive death-grip for 33 minutes.

Every man was a hero in defence while the fleeting forwards of Liverpool probed restlessly, keeping Freddie Cox's men at full stretch.

Then Hateley, soccer's most costly reserve for the last five weeks, struck to bring a breath of life to Liverpool.

Bill Shankly had brought him back to add more punch to the attack that failed to score in Saturday's drawn game at Bournemouth.

It paid a golden dividend as Hateley thundered one of his typical headers into the far corner of the net from a Tommy Smith cross.

And the Bournemouth defence suddenly started to tear apart as easily as a page of perforated stamps. Peter Thompson burst through to make it 2—0 two minutes later with a shot that spun out of goalkeeper Roger Jones's hands.

Overworked

Roger Hunt made it 3—0 after 57 minutes, then Chris Lawler moved through the overworked Bournemouth defence to score No. 4 in the 74th minute.

Yet Bournemouth's honest endeavour won them the hearts of the Kop fans and the loudest cheer of the night went up when Emlyn Hughes turned the ball into his own net with three Bournemouth forwards on his heels.

Consolation for Bournemouth? They will take home around £5,000—their share of the cash paid by last night's capacity crowd of 54,071.

How they deserve it! Just as they deserve the cheers they got at the end as they walked out of the Cup with their heads held high.

The young fans followed them towards the dressing rooms waving a huge banner that carried a fitting epitaph.

It read simply : " Tony Hateley —King of the Air "

David Stocks goes for the ball after Roger Hunt and Tommy Naylor, both on the ground, had had a heading duel.

Ian St. John, Liverpool's Scottish schemer, who had such a fine replay game, controls the ball as Bumstead prepares to tackle. Stocks is ready to intercept. First game pictures by staff cameramen Ron Morley and Roland Evans.

The two rematches with Liverpool were personal career highlights. (Bournemouth Daily Echo)

(Above) The programmes from my rematches with Liverpool.
(Left: AFC Bournemouth, right: Liverpool FC)

MacDougall scores twice but misses that magic 50

*(Above) Celebrating promotion!
Almost certainly the best moment of
my career. (Bournemouth Daily Echo)*

*(Right) Bournemouth & Boscombe
no longer: kitted out in red and black
as part of the AFC Bournemouth
rebrand. (AFC Bournemouth)*

*The first team squad under John Bond in the new strip, trying to emulate AC Milan!
(AFC Bournemouth)*

STOCKS SIGNS —BUT STAYS

BOSCOMBE full-back David Stocks, after lengthy negotiations, signed for Torquay United at a fee of about £2,500, and was due to play for his new club at Oldham today. Part of the agreement was that he should continue to live in Bournemouth.

The 27-year-old Stocks, former Gillingham and Charlton Athletic player, started last season as skipper of the Boscombe side and missed only seven of the league fixtures during the Cherries' promotion run in the Fourth Division.

He was signed by the Dean Court club in June, 1966, at the same time as Tommy Taylor—now with Poole Town—in a deal that also took winger Charlie Crickmore to Gillingham.

Stocks, a qualified FA coach, has totalled 245 first team appearances and, until this season when he dropped out of the side following an injury, has been a regular in the line-up.

DAVID STOCKS

His consistency during the last few seasons included an unbroken sequence of 149 appearances and in that five-year spell of solid service he missed only a handful of matches.

(Left) You wouldn't see this happening too many times now! (Bournemouth Daily Echo)

(Right) Leading out Torquay. (Colin Bratcher, Herald Express)

(Below) In my Torquay kit, back when I had hair! (Author's own collection)

Signing for Torquay, and more proof of my goalscoring prowess! (Herald Express)

HEADS UP —STOCKS MAKES IT

Torquay 1, Bolton 1
A BRILLIANT fortieth-minute goal by Bolton left back Don McAllister injected some life into what had been a dull game at Torquay.

Torquay, doomed to Fourth Division football next season, then turned on some explosive forward play and 'keeper Charlie Wright was at full stretch to save from Bruce Stuckey.

Wright was lucky to turn away what looked a sure goal for Dave Teasue, but the Bolton goalkeeper could not keep out a Dave Stocks header for Torquay's equaliser in the fifty-ninth minute.

RESULTS

FIRST DIVISION

Torquay signs Dave Stocks

Full-back Dave Stocks joined Torquay this week for a £5,000 fee. Formerly with Charlton and Gillingham, Stocks came to Dean Court in the closed season of 1966 and played over 250 first-team matches for the Cherries.

(Left) Sorry Steve! Tangling with Steve Gritt when I returned to Dean Court with Torquay (Panda Soft Drinks Ltd, Blandford)

(Below) Pre-season training around the back at Plainmoor! (Colin Bratcher, Herald Express)

Torquay lose Stocks with double fracture

Dave Stocks

Lincoln City ... 4   Torquay United ... 2
(Ward, Fleming,   (Twitchin, Boulton)
Brandfoot, Freeman)   Att. 4,128

TORQUAY UNITED crashed to their first defeat of the season against a powerful Lincoln side yesterday. They never recovered from the early loss of defender Dave Stocks — carried off with a double fracture of the lower right leg after only five minutes.

Although they went in at the interval level at 2-2, City turned on the pressure in the second half to score twice and romp home.

United have, in fact, young keeper Terry Lee to thank for conceding only four goals. He produced a string of brilliant saves to keep the wayward home forwards at bay.

Things started badly for United with Stocks going down after a tackle with

by JIM MARTIN

home defender Dennis Leigh.

After five minutes' treatment on the field he was carried off. He broke his leg once before at the end of the 1973-74 season at Newport.

Cliff Myers moved into the back four and substitute

Ian Twitchin came into midfield.

United took time to settle down, and for the first half hour it was all Lincoln.

Man of the match John Fleming shot narrowly wide after twelve minutes. Lee brilliantly turned aside a Dick Krzywicki shot a minute later then the keeper dived full length to keep out a header from City skipper Sam Ellis.

But after 31 minutes—during which time Torquay had hardly managed to raise an attack—City took the lead.

Peter Graham chipped a

ball into the middle, defender Pat Kruse deflected the ball beyond Lee, and City striker John Ward followed up to grab his fifth goal in two matches.

This stung United into action and three minutes later they grabbed a shock equaliser. Full-back Phil Sandercock pushed Ellis to send over a centre, and with the Lincoln defence looking on, substitute Twitchin bent low to head it into the net from eight yards.

Immediately the home side hit back and Alan Harding beat Lee with a fierce shot only to see the ball hit the bar and bounce back into play.

But after 42 minutes City regained the lead. Lee and Gerbic blocked Ward's close-range drive, the ball ran loose and when Krzywicki centred it was headed for Fleming to drive home from 15 yards.

Torquay, though, snatched an equaliser in the fifth minute of injury time after an Andy Provan corner. The home defence failed to clear the ball and Clint Boulton rammed home his third goal of the season from close range.

Saved

United started the second half with more aggression and Ian Brandfoot saved a dangerous situation by Lincoln by pushing the ball out for a corner as Twitchin closed in.

And after 50 minutes they missed a great chance of

taking the lead. Provan pushing a ball through the middle, and when Ellis mis-kicked Willie Brown was left with a clear run at goal. But he pushed the ball too far forward and keeper Peter Grotier was easily able to save.

Lee was soon back in action magnificently pulling down Ward's chipped drive after the striker had shocked beat Twitchin.

Headed

Myers saved a dangerous situation for Torquay after 62 minutes when he headed the ball for a corner after Lee had only just saved Ward's shot.

City brought on Percy Freeman for Graham and within three minutes took the lead. Ellis returned a cleared corner into the middle and Brandfoot, standing on the line, headed home.

There were protests from Torquay players before the re-start and referee P. Telfer, of Dudley, appeared to book both Twitchin and Boulton.

Lincoln kept up the pressure and Freeman forced Lee into a fine save at the other end David Kennedy went close with a fierce drive.

City wrapped matters up with a goal four minutes from time. Fleming and Freeman through and with the United defence wide open the big striker had plenty of time to shoot past Lee.

Laid up with a broken leg courtesy of a late tackle in an away defeat at Lincoln, together with the papers report on the match and my injury.
(Colin Bratcher, Herald Express)

DAVE THOMAS

It could hardly have begun in more daunting circumstances—the league career of Dave Stocks.

On a Saturday in the spring of 1961, Liverpool played their last match in the Second Division in front of 54,000 fans at Anfield. They won the championship by eight points from Leyton Orient. And that was the day Charlton chose to give 18-year-old Stocks his debut. "I was terrified," he said simply. His understandable fear was not to last long. For fear was one word that no one could link with Dave over the next 16 years—although some of his opponents may have felt the odd twinge!

He played 442 league games for Charlton, Gillingham, Bournemouth and Torquay and would certainly have topped the 500-mark but for suffering two broken legs during his Plainmoor career.

The second, and worst, break was at Sincil Bank just over two years ago. United were causing Lincoln City considerable embarrassment when Dave went into a tackle with an opponent who had better remain nameless. Dave, great tackler that he was, went in hard and honest as always. He made contact, kicked through the ball and his right leg cracked against the studs of an outstretched boot.

It is easy to recall the reaction of the United players when we went to collect Dave from the local hospital. Their efforts to cheer him up could not hide the anger and sadness they felt inside. But Dave stresses now: "What really annoys me was that the break didn't cause my retirement. I recovered from that—although it was a bad break. It was an ankle injury that forced me to stop—a silly old ankle injury."

The United fans soon saw what everyone at Plainmoor feared—that the loss of Stocks had taken a big chunk of the team's heart away. He was the sort of defender for whom managers thank their lucky stars. He would run out on a miserable day at Workington, joking that this was no place for class players, and then prove over 90 minutes that he was absolutely right.

United bought him from Bournemouth, where he had helped John Bond's side to promotion, in January, 1972. He cost a ridiculous £2,000. He arrived as a left-back, but soon moved inside and wore a No.6 shirt for most of his Plainmoor career. He was a master tackler, a genuinely skilful player on the ball and read the game so well that he was seldom caught out on the turn. He affectionately referred to his left foot as "The Scythe", but that was doing himself less than justice.

As well as being a model professional in his job, Dave has always been an intelligent and likeable man off it. He is now making a success in his new profession in the insurance and investment field. "I never remembered what it was like to work hard!" he says now.

And when he looks back on those 16 years, he might just take pride in a small thought from that first appearance at Anfield. The man he marked was a winger by the name of Ian Callaghan.

Two better pros never graced the Football League.

The notes and tickets for my testimonial programme. A great write-up by Dave Thomas. (Author's own collection)

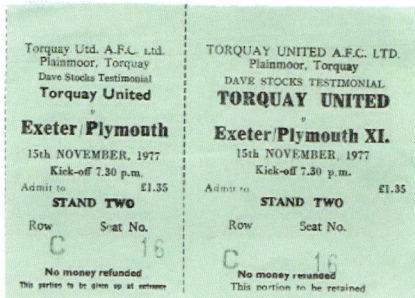

Cricket club may sponsor soccer man Dave

BARTON Cricket Club are pleased to have Torquay United footballer Dave Stocks in their team. And to prove it they are thinking of sponsoring him in the next soccer season.

Barton aim to ask members at their Cricketfield Road clubhouse to donate money towards a £25 total to sponsor Dave's soccer strip when he turns out for United.

They will be paying £15 for his boots, £6 for his shirt, £3 for his shorts and £1 for each of his socks.

Their reward for the sponsorship will be to have their name published each week in the United programme.

Barton secretary Mike Braund told the News: "The feeling of most members is that Barton should sponsor their own player in Dave Stocks.

"The plan has to be approved by the committee but everybody's for it and there should be no problems."

United boss Malcolm Musgrove was pleased to hear that the local cricket club are thinking of sponsoring Dave.

United decided to set up the sponsorship plan after neighbours Plymouth Argyle had made a successful go of it last season.

The Plainmoor scheme is heading for success as well. Five other players have been sponsored, including Jimmy Dunne, Pat Kruse, Terry Lee, Phil Sandercock and Willie Brown.

Mr Musgrove sees no difficulty in finding people to put their names to the kits of the other 10 players at Plainmoor.

"We should get sponsers for every player without difficulty. Six organisations have already paid the £25 sponsorship and we have numerous other promises as well," says Mr Musgrove.

★ ★ ★

DAVE STOCKS has killed two birds with one stone by joining Barton Cricket Club this season. Not only has he considerably helped his comeback chances with Torquay United next season by keeping fit playing cricket, but now Barton have decided to sponsor his playing kit.

At the end of last season United launched a Sponsorkit Scheme, in which individuals or groups of supporters can pay for playing equipment of their favourite players.

Barton members have decided to chip in to a fund to meet the £25 cost of the shirt, shorts, socks and boots which Dave will wear next winter.

Dave said: "After being out for so long with my broken leg, I know that competition for places will be fiercer for me than most, but this news is a big boost. It makes me all the more determined to get back in that first-team."

Other United players who have been backed under the scheme so far are Player Of The Year Pat Kruse, last season's leading scorer Willie Brown, new signing Jimmy Dunne, P.F.A. Fourth Division left-back Phil Sandercock and goalkeeper Terry Lee.

★ ★ ★

CHARLTON FOOTBALLER NEARS 100 WICKETS

DAVID STOCKS, young Charlton full-back, has pulled off some fine performances as a bowler in club cricket this summer, and has a chance of reaching a hundred wickets in a season for the first time.

Fair-haired David took eight wickets for 60 runs for Harvey's Sports Club against Old Shootershillians at Hervey Road on Monday.

Last week, at Stone's sports ground, Stocks hit 52 runs not out for Charlton footballers against Greenwich Police, and then took 4 wickets for 16 runs in seven overs.

A FINE TOTAL

Batting first against the police, Charlton hit up 231 in one hour 50 minutes before declaring with six wickets down.

Only right-winger Michael Kenning failed to reach double figures. The score were: Brian Tocknell 18, Brian Kinsey 27, Cliff Durandt 30, Keith Peacock 37, Dennis Edwards 39, Kenning 3, David Stocks 52 not out, Michael Rose 20 not out.

HIT EIGHT FOURS

Stocks scored his 52 runs in less than half-an-hour and hit eight boundaries. Edwards scored six fours, and Durandt five.

Greenwich Police were tumbled out for 69, their best scores being Wood (15), Cooper (16) and Sumner (14).

Wicket takers for Charlton were Stocks 4 for 16, Edwards 3 for 9, Manager Frank Hill 2 for 4, and trainer "Jock" Basford 1 for 2.

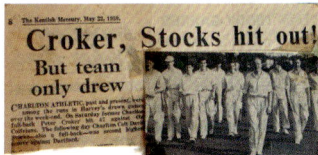

The Kentish Mercury, May 22, 1959.

Croker, Stocks hit out!
But team only drew

CHARLTON ATHLETIC, past and present, held among the run in Harvey's drawn game...

(Left) Taking my Sunday league captaincy seriously. (Author's own collection)

(Right) No discipline in the local league – it's my ball! (Author's own collection)

The motley crew of the G&T Wednesday afternoon team, featuring none other than Mr T himself, Tony Sword (front row, far right) as well as local hotelier brothers, Simon and Dave Young (second and third from left, back row) and Rickie Summers, brother of Andy of The Police fame (middle front row). (Author's own collection)

the reserves and juniors. There wouldn't be much in the way of real coaching, and the match could drag on for anything up to two hours. Sometimes the manager would place some of the first team players with the reserves, the thinking behind this being to let him know that he may be dropped and subsequently motivate him to work harder. When this happened to me, which it often did, I did indeed try a bit harder, normally resulting in me as a left-back making some fairly rough tackles on my opposing winger, who would sometimes be a young junior apprentice. It became quite a joke in the dressing room, as it was often a young, innocent new signing receiving his welcome to the club and the world of professional football! It was an interesting psychological approach, but I would invariably be back in the first team lineup the following Saturday.

Interestingly, following a conversation with a good friend of mine, Steve Webb, who was a junior player at the time, he recalls jumping away from some of the tackles dished out by yours truly in these games. I am not sure in today's football world whether this would be acceptable, but time and training techniques move on, and not necessarily in the right direction.

Thursday

Back to training behind the stand – very few clubs at our level had training grounds. Sometimes we would use a local sports ground, or even a park so we could train on grass, much to the amusement of the local dog walkers. On occasion, we would take advantage of being close to the coast and use the beach or promenade between Bournemouth and Boscombe piers. Some of the players, myself included, would do extra training on our own. For example, afterwards we would do extra shooting practice on the main pitch, assuming weather conditions were good and it wouldn't damage the pitch, although the groundsman didn't like us using it, as it was his pride and joy!

Practice would consist of balls being fired into the penalty area, where the likes of MacDougall and Boyer would finish off the crosses. I remember when Ted first arrived at the club, and it was very evident that he could finish well. I asked him what was on his mind when he was in front of goal, and his reply was interesting. He said that he would normally like to leave space in front of goal so that when he made contact with the ball, he was on the move, which in itself generated power on the ball. He would ask the player crossing the ball or passing through to him to play it as early as possible. He would then leave the space to run onto. This sounds very simple, but he would spend hours honing his technique. They say that practice makes perfect, and for Ted it certainly did.

One interesting piece of insight he imparted was that when he was in front of goal and about to shoot, he told me that everything went into slow motion, and he was able to finish in a calm and deliberate way. This was a gift, and made him in my opinion one of the best finishers in the country – very reminiscent of Jimmy Greaves in his prime, but more physical, with extra pace and certainly a better header of the ball.

Friday

This would be a strange day, with different managers having different approaches. Some would do as little as possible – just a warm-up and a few sprints, with no work with the ball, the reason being that it was thought that the team would then be hungry for the ball come Saturday. I wasn't sure about that philosophy personally, but believe me, it happened!

Others would put on a gentle running warm-up and a short ball-work session to get the touch and feel without too much exertion the day before the match. This was the approach that I preferred. There would normally be a meeting after the training session where the make-up of the team was confirmed and a few tactical issues discussed, mainly about the shape and details of some of the opposition players. Generally, there was not a great deal of information, unlike today with the high volume of detail available on the opposition.

During the week there was no advice on diet and lifestyle; you were left to your own routine. Basically, there were simple rules stating that we were not allowed out to pubs and clubs after Wednesday. If anyone was caught breaking this rule then they would be fined. After the match itself, the players were allowed alcoholic drinks, and we would normally have a beer or two in the club bar with the supporters and some of the opposition. If we were playing away, sometimes we would be allowed to stop for a beer, but in most cases we would head straight back on the coach, especially if we had lost.

Treatment for any injuries was handled by Arthur

Cunliffe in the formidable treatment room. There was one occasion that Steve Webb reminded me of when he was in the treatment room to have a blister removed – with the aid of a scalpel – which was being done by the bucket-and-sponge man! Considering that Cunliffe would also stop us from drinking cold water, saying that it was bad for us, he didn't exactly inspire confidence on the treatment front!

I was being treated for a dead thigh with an electrode device of some sort – don't ask me the technical name for it. A few of my teammates (I'm reliably informed that they were John Sainty, Micky Cave, David Jones and Tony Powell) came larking about. At this point, one of them decided that it would be hilarious to turn up the charge, causing my leg to start jumping all over the treatment bed. Fortunately there was no lasting damage!

Saturday

Match day. For home matches we slept at home the night before the game. For away matches we would stay at a hotel where we were playing on the Friday night. We were allocated double rooms, sharing with one of our teammates. We weren't given any specific dietary advice for Friday night, and Saturday morning breakfast at the hotel was usually toast and/or cereal, followed by a short walk outside to stretch our legs before lunch at around noon. Lunch would be steak and toast, or just toast and a cup of tea – not sure steak was the best preparation meal before a match! This was discussed a number of times, the result being that eventually it was changed to chicken, which was not quite so heavy in the stomach.

We would arrive at the ground around an hour and a half before kick-off, sign a few autographs on the way to the changing rooms, and get kitted out. We didn't do much of a warm-up before the game; we just ran out and kicked a ball about for a few minutes before the whistle – a far cry from today's routines. I personally made a bit more of an effort to warm up in the changing room by kicking a ball against the side of the communal bath or a wall, along with a few stretches. I think the back-up staff at clubs today would have a heart attack at the lack of preparation by the players back then!

Nowadays at half time, the players are given various drinks to rehydrate – back then we had a cup of tea. On this I would opt out, as it actually made me feel sick, so I went without fluids for the whole game. Afterwards there was the ritual of the communal hot bath and a beer. I'm not sure how that would go down today, although the thought of an ice bath after a match at Hartlepool on a cold winter's day fills me with dread. We would grab a sandwich or something similar for the journey home if at an away match – there were no recovery drinks back then. My general eating habits were better than most, but we weren't really guided or advised on nutrition like the clubs do now. It is quite amazing how the game has changed, but with so much money at stake, it makes sense to implement changes that will improve performance and reduce injuries.

When you look back to the matches from the '60s and '70s, there is a huge difference in the standard of play. There are still top-quality players with similar skills to those of the past – the difference is the physicality and speed at which the game is played. Tactically, there has been a huge increase in awareness, but ultimately it's still a game with 22 players on the pitch.

When you have a squad of players that get on well, good results often tend to follow. Teamwork is vital in any team sport, and if you get a change of management as a football club, this sometimes results in changes to the squad, and fitting new recruits into an existing team is not an easy task. Any new players will be replacing existing members of the team, which can create an atmosphere, but winning matches inevitably solves this issue, hence the requirement for managers and coaches with man-management skills as well as coaching ability.

-

Prior to the start of the 1971/72 season, the good times seemed to be just around the corner. After working really hard throughout the summer on my fitness (around a dozen of us turned up early for pre-season), I came into the first match half a stone lighter, and was playing the best football of my life. An injury to Mel Machin meant I started the season in the back four alongside John Benson, Tony Powell and new signing Bill Kitchener (another former teammate of Bond's from West Ham). Benson was a good defensive partner – thoughtful and committed, he was very analytical about the game, and it didn't surprise me that he went into management. I was actually quite surprised that his spell in charge at Bournemouth didn't really work out for him.

Our return to the Third Division couldn't have gone much better: an opening-day 3-1 victory against Shrewsbury at Dean Court was followed by a goalless draw at Bolton and further home victories against Rotherham and Blackburn. Unfortunately, as often tends to happen in situations like this, bad luck intervened. Following a 1-0 defeat away at Halifax, I got injured in a 4-1 win over Rochdale when I was clattered, and that was it for me. I was out for two months.

The injury was to my knee – torn ligaments – which was hugely disappointing, as at the time I was playing with the confidence of someone who had just won promotion and was benefiting from a new training regime. I wanted to be part of that team. But that's football; it can be very cruel at times. Once I had recovered from my injury, it became clear that Bond did not see me as part of the team's future. I was still part of the first team squad, but got next to no game time. My left-back spot was covered by a number of different players, such as Powell, Miller, Kitchener and Bobby Howe – all of whom, with the exception of Powell, were recruited from Bond's old club, West Ham.

It became clear that the future style and recruitment of players would be very much in the West Ham mould. Those of us from the past were discarded in the main, apart from the likes of Ted MacDougall and Phil Boyer, who both went on to write themselves into Cherries folklore. It was certainly a time of change, the style of play moving from a mainly defensive approach to a more attacking style. The game plan was that if the opposition scored three, we'd score four – and with Ted in the side, there was always a reasonable chance of that. Playing mainly in the reserves for Bournemouth was not what I wanted at this stage of my career. We were now halfway through the 1971/72 season, and at the age of 28 I was at another crossroads. Do I look for another club and continue with my football career, or should I look to go back to a 'normal' job and use the qualifications I had gained in my earlier years?

By this point, I had made a total of 245 appearances, with just two goals: the one against Southport, and the other in the relegation season in a 2-1 reverse at Torquay United. This would be far from the last I would be seeing of this particular club...

SIX

OFF TO THE ENGLISH RIVIERA

I was aware of rumours that a few clubs were interested in signing me. Brighton, QPR, Portsmouth and Brentford had all been mooted, plus a few northern clubs (these were never serious options for me due to the distance involved). This was a very difficult time for me, my experiences to date showing just how cut-throat the football world could be. At this point, players moved almost at the whim of their clubs. The directors and managers were only interested in success, almost at any cost, and if we're honest, the supporters too would rather have been winning. Managers in particular were under enormous pressure to provide results, as they still are.

Little did I know that a solution to my predicament was just around the corner. During the last few weeks of the season, scouts from Torquay United – then managed by Jack Edwards – had been watching me play for the reserves. I had faced them several times over the past few years in what at the time was the closest thing to a local derby for Bournemouth (even though we are over a hundred miles apart).

They were in the same division as Bournemouth, albeit at the bottom end of the table. A number of our players had previously played for them, such as Bill Kitchener, Micky Cave, Tony Scott and John Benson, plus of course John Bond, so there was an obvious connection between the clubs. I first had an inkling that something was up when Bond asked to see me. "I want to talk to you about your position at Bournemouth," he said. Oh, right. Perhaps naively, I thought that it might be to discuss a new contract. Not quite.

"I'm selling you. You're going to Torquay."

What? "No I'm not."

"Yes you are, you're going."

"No, I'm not going. I don't want to go. Why should I go?"

"Well it's no good staying here, because I'm not going to play you."

That was that. A couple months later, he called me in to tell me that Torquay had come back with an increased offer, and that he wanted me to go.

At this point I had been out of the team for a while, and couldn't see the point in staying, so off I went to discuss a move. I wanted first-team football, and with Torquay in the same league, it didn't feel like a step down. This was to become a complex series of negotiations, as I did not want to relocate to Torquay at this time, enjoying my side hustle of working at Castle Court School as a sports coach.

In an interesting twist of fate, my connection to Castle Court was renewed later on when my two sons, Oliver and Alexander, ended up studying there.

A well-run private school, the Castle Court experience made quite an impact on me. The head teacher at the time was Mr Donald Scott – very much a disciplinarian, but a charming man. Taking part in coaching – and sometimes being involved in lessons – it opened my eyes to this level of education. I had of course undertaken some sports coaching at various London state schools while playing for Charlton and Gillingham during the afternoons after training, but that was not at the levels expected at Castle Court.

Unlike when I was coaching in London, here a lot of the pupils knew who I was. Kids being kids, I inevitably got a bit of backchat, but in the main they were very respectful, as they appreciated that as a professional footballer, I probably knew what I was talking about. I even did a bit of tennis and cricket coaching – I wasn't just a one-trick pony! Funnily enough, when Ollie and Alex went to school there in the 2000s, it turned out that their sports teacher, as well as some of the parents, had been taught by me. It was great to reminisce about old times with them.

My time at Castle Court also renewed my acquaintance with the head of sport, Michael Wheeler. Having made initial contact with Mike via his involvement in training at Bournemouth as an occasional fitness coach, he recommended me to the school as a coach. His influence on me was quite strong – he was an incredible athlete and a natural runner. Nobody at the club could compete with him. In fact, when taking training, he would continue to talk to us while running, and even our best athletes, the likes of Terry Gulliver, Tony Powell and Ted MacDougall, couldn't keep up. Through his training, he helped us to improve our running by changing our techniques and breathing, which made a significant difference to our fitness and recovery in match situations.

-

Anyway, back to Torquay. Ultimately, a deal was agreed that I was to live and train in Bournemouth, which enabled me to continue to coach and teach at Castle Court in the afternoons, and train with the reserves and juniors at Dean Court during the mornings. I was happy to do this, as it fitted in with my plans.

The main issue was the amount of travelling – not only to Torquay for home matches, but arranging to get to the away matches scattered all over the country, especially the ones up north: the likes of Doncaster, Scunthorpe and, worst of all, Darlington and Hartlepool. I had in the past overcome many difficulties in my career, and I was used to accommodating travel issues. Even back in my Charlton days as a youngster, I overcame the issues of having two occupations, and it looked as though I would have to work something out again, only on a much larger scale. After all, it's a long way from Bournemouth to Torquay, never mind the away matches around the country!

Torquay as a football club was way off the radar for

most professional footballers. It was – and is – a beautiful town with a great climate, way down in the south west of England. This was exactly its problem. Its location is almost off the map in the footballing world, and with home crowds at the time averaging less than three thousand, it was not exactly a hotbed of football. Its nearest neighbours were Exeter City and Plymouth Argyle, around 25 and 30 miles away respectively.

After several visits to the area and lengthy discussions regarding my contract, a transfer fee of £2,000 was agreed between the clubs. To both put this into perspective and make an ever so slight understatement, the financial side of the game for players back in 1972 was somewhat different to what it is today. My contract was for 18 months from 20th January 1972 to 30th June 1974, and the basic wage was £40 a week, with £5 a week extra when playing or substitute for league matches. There was also a £10 bonus per point if we got promoted.

Having been involved in a number of transfers by this point, I knew the ropes, and was able to negotiate a handsome signing-on fee for myself. In addition to the levy of £83.33 payable on 30th June of 1972, 1973 and 1974, there was a service bonus of £500 payable on these dates. It was also agreed that I could continue to reside in Bournemouth, and would receive 'reasonable travelling expenses' when journeying between Bournemouth and Torquay, as well as to and from away matches.

On top of this, there was participation in a pool, not exceeding 20 per cent of the club's net receipts for FA Cup matches at the discretion of the directors, plus £5 per appearance in the FA Cup first round, £10 for the second round, £17 for the third, £25 for the fourth and £38 for the fifth. The important factor here was that contractually I would be allowed to continue residing in Bournemouth, allowing my family to not have to relocate, especially as I was training with Bournemouth's reserve and junior squads, and had a three-year-old son. I could continue my work at Castle Court, but it was not easy to reconcile all of this with the travelling required for home and away matches. For instance, in the event of a mid-week home match, I would train at Bournemouth in the morning, coach at Castle Court in the afternoon and then get away as early as possible and drive to Torquay.

I would head to my digs, which were just around the corner from the ground, as I would often stay over and drive back to Bournemouth the next day. If I did this, I would head straight to Castle Court for the coaching session in the afternoon. I am not sure that this kind of deal would be allowed today, especially with the traffic that is now on the roads and the obvious requirement for rest and diet. Back then I was effectively living the life of a long-distance lorry driver, eating at motorway cafes and getting very little rest. It was incredible that it actually worked!

The Saturday home matches were easier: Torquay normally played in the evening at 7.30pm, so I would drive down during the day and stay over on Saturday night after the match. This allowed me to have a night out with my teammates. However, when there was a change in management, with Malcolm Musgrove taking over from

Jack Edwards, I was asked to come down on the Thursday night, train with the team on Friday morning, and then go back home on Saturday after the match.

The logistics for away matches were more complicated: on Saturdays, most games were in the Midlands, or more northerly at places like Oldham, Barnsley, Blackburn, Halifax and Wrexham. I did not want to drive to Torquay, then travel all the way up to the match on the coach and then back to Torquay, and then have to drive back to Bournemouth. Consequently, the arrangement was agreed that I would either drive directly to the ground from Bournemouth when playing teams such as Aston Villa, Brighton and Bristol Rovers, while for the more northerly clubs, I would meet the coach on the M5 motorway at Strensham service station at an agreed time. I would leave my car in the car park, travel with the team by coach, stay over with the team on the Friday night, and play in the game on Saturday. I would then get dropped off there on the way back, hoping that my car would still be where I left it, and have all its wheels! I would then drive back to Bournemouth and meet up with some of my old teammates – usually Terry Gulliver and goalkeeper Kim Book – for a few drinks.

Looking back, I still can't believe that I actually kept this up for half a season, but I was not the only player at Torquay who had this kind of arrangement – quite often, thanks to their geographical location, it helped them to recruit new players.

-

My first match for Torquay was away at Oldham on 22nd January 1972, where we won 1-0. I managed to play 45 of the 46 games that season, missing only the Exeter home game through injury – coincidentally, Torquay lost 2-0. The rivalry between the clubs was very intense, with the home and away ties that season drawing crowds of 8,164 and 11,296 respectively. We lost both matches, going down 2-3 in the away fixture, but the crowds were amazing, as our average home gate would generally be between two and three thousand.

When I joined part way through the season, Torquay were in the bottom four, so it came as no surprise that at the end of the 1971/72 season, we were relegated after finishing second from bottom. I did wonder what I had let myself in for, but I was still keen to have a career in football for a few more years if I could. I knew what to expect as far as the lower standard went, but playing first team football on a regular basis was nice after so long without it, and they were a great set of lads to play with.

The manager at the time, Jack Edwards, was a pleasant guy, but to my mind he lacked the skills needed to manage a football team. He was easy to get on with, but lacked personality and I always felt he didn't have the requisite cutting edge. Ultimately, Malcolm Musgrove replaced him midway through the following season. He was a different kind of manager to Jack – having only just started in management, he was enthusiastic and arrived with some very modern ideas for training and playing. However, he found it difficult to make do with the limited resources on offer at a lower league club. He was very approachable as a manager, and ultimately his various connections allowed him to make some decent signings.

The slog of travelling to and from Bournemouth and the added difficulty of getting to the away games started to take its toll on me both physically and mentally. I didn't really feel part of the team like I had at my previous clubs, but financially it had worked out quite well, even if I didn't get as many win bonuses as I would have liked! At times though, I wasn't sure where I should be. It seemed like my life was being almost entirely spent driving to training, playing matches, coaching and then briefly returning home. With the additional income, I decided to upgrade my car, and purchased a second-hand MGB GT – a nice treat, but why not, what with all the time I was spending in the car. However, it didn't turn out to be the best decision I made, as it wasn't that comfortable on long journeys, and being second hand, it was in the garage regularly for repair works.

On one occasion, I had a problem with the spokes in one of the wheels and had to call in at a garage near Sherborne to look at the clicking noise coming from one of the wheels. The mechanic who fixed the wheel was brilliant, but he could not believe I was on my way to rendezvous with the team at Strensham for our away match at Rochdale.

It soon became evident that something had to change. By this point I had been appointed club captain, and in August 1973 I agreed to move to Torquay to live, and signed a new contract, with a basic wage comprising the princely sum of £40 per week, which was a good salary back then. I also agreed to purchase the property I was renting. It was owned by the then chairman, Tony Boyce, who was a local solicitor/businessman, which was handy when it came to all the legal work needed for the house purchase. The club was very keen to recruit players of a good standard, but needed to go above and beyond in order to entice players to relocate so far south.

-

Having finished 18th in the Fourth Division during the 1972/73 season (after being relegated the previous year), hopes were high for the following campaign, but as they say, football is a funny old game. I completed a full pre-season programme in Torquay with several new signings. I had taken on the number six shirt as a central defender, and was now playing alongside Derek Harrison, a commanding centre-half signed from Leicester.

The opening match was away to Bury, and we were brought down to earth with a bang by a 4-0 defeat – not the best of starts. Playing in the Fourth Division again was proving to be physically demanding, to put it mildly. While the players often couldn't quite match those higher up the league on a technical level, they were more than happy to use their physical strength to make up for this. I was still adjusting to this, and visits to the likes of Lincoln, Barnsley, Workington and other northern sides were thus quite intimidating. Us soft southerners from the south coast of Devon were seen as a good target for their bullying.

It didn't take me long, however, to think back to my time at Gillingham and rediscover how to dish out the physical side of the game. This very quickly spread through the team, and we became a much harder team to play against – it was very much a case of needs must. Little did I know that there was trouble just around the corner.

Away to Newport County on 3rd February 1974 was not a match that would draw much attention – a crowd of just 3,480 witnessed a 2-2 draw, but it would prove to be eventful for me in a different way. Upon clearing a ball from our penalty, a Newport player took it upon himself to go in late on me. It looked like an innocuous enough challenge, but I knew there was a problem. A feeling of excruciating pain just below my knee suggested something serious, but I thought, "Never mind, it will be fine." However, it turned out that putting any weight on my leg hurt, so with that my game was over.

When we got back to Torquay, I was dropped off at home. On the Monday morning, I went off to the hospital for a precautionary x-ray, which showed a small fracture in my left leg. My season was over – I was put in a plaster cast from the ankle to thigh, although the doctor reassured me that I should be okay for the following season.

In those days there were no structured rehabilitation programmes – at least, there weren't at Torquay – so the next few months were spent sitting on my backside twiddling my thumbs, unable to drive; just hobbling around. I had evaded major injuries throughout my career up to this point, so this was an unwelcome new experience for me. After a few weeks, a shorter plaster was put on, which did enable me to regain some mobility. It was all very frustrating, having played in every one of the 31 games prior to the injury. The team ended the season 16th in the table.

-

I spent the close season training to make sure I was available for the start of the 1974/75 season. Malcolm Musgrove confirmed that he wanted me to start the season once more as one of the central defenders. This was fine with me, as I continued to have a great partner in Derek Harrison, who was an excellent header of the ball. I was there to read the game and organise the defence, which suited me at this stage in my career. The start to the season wasn't great – a 3-0 defeat at home to Rotherham – but the crowd was an encouraging 4,020. I joked that they had all turned up to see my return to the team!

We followed this up with a run of five unbeaten games, and later in the season I scored against Chester – something that was most unusual for me, as I was normally not allowed in the opposition penalty area. My finishing was, and still is, appalling, but I was back with a bang, and managed to play in every one of the 46 games that season.

The team finished the season in a very respectable 14th with 42 points. Mansfield Town were champions with 68 points, six points clear of Shrewsbury Town in second. Unfortunately, we failed at the first hurdle in the FA Cup and Football League Cup, losing 1-0 on both occasions to Northampton and Newport County respectively.

Having played every game in the 1974/75 season, I was in high spirits, and looking forward to the coming season. Towards the end of the year, we signed a powerful centre-half, Pat Kruse, from Leicester as a replacement for Harrison, who unfortunately acquired a career-ending injury. Kruse and I played the last ten games together, winning seven of them. We complemented each other well – he was powerful in the air and very mobile on the ground, so with my experience alongside him, as well as the two full-backs, Phil Sandercock and Ian Twitchin, we were collectively a very formidable back four.

The 1975/76 season looked very promising, thanks to the introduction of our new player-coach, Lew Chatterley from Aston Villa, and Musgrove was having a positive impact. We also brought in goalkeeper Terry Lee from Tottenham and seasoned goalscorer Willie Brown from Brentford. With Kruse and I at the back, the spine of the team looked very solid.

On 16th August 1975, we navigated the first game at home to Workington with a 1-0 victory, during which, a second-half penalty from Phil Sandercock secured the victory. Next up was away at Lincoln City on 23rd August. Sadly, my hopes of maintaining this great start were dashed when disaster struck 20 minutes in with the score at 0-0. I went into a tackle with one of the Lincoln forwards on the halfway line – in those days the game was much more physical than now, and challenges were certainly more robust. It was a 50/50 challenge, but my opponent (who shall remain nameless) went over the top of the ball with his studs, which collided with my shin. The result was a double break of both tibia and fibula just above the right ankle, and a trip to hospital in Lincoln.

My leg was duly plastered from ankle to thigh, and while this obviously wasn't the most pleasant experience, I must say that the care and treatment I received was superb. I was given an anaesthetic, and woke up in plaster. Should I stay in hospital overnight? "No" was the answer – the coach that took us to Lincoln picked me up from the hospital. I was carried onto the coach by the other players, and put on the back seat for the journey back to Torquay. We lost 4-2, by the way!

Once in Torquay, the coach dropped me off at home. Two of the players carried me to my house, and the next day the club doctor visited me and basically said, "Oh, that's a shame, it's both bones fractured, you will be in plaster for six months." Great, I thought. What was I going to do with myself for the rest of the season?

Even though I was going to be out for the rest of the campaign, I would still be paid my salary – just not any bonuses. We weren't winning a lot of matches anyway, so it became a case of preparing to make a comeback at the beginning of the next season, 1976/77. My contract would run through to include that season, but this was all assuming my leg healed properly, and that I would be capable of playing at that level again. It was a matter of waiting to find out, and patience is not one of my strengths.

I received many get-well wishes from friends, family, teammates and supporters, which was very encouraging and supportive. I actually still have the programme from that game, covered with white powder from the plaster cast!

-

During the rest of the season, the team did fairly well without me, finishing in a credible ninth position. Interestingly, the third from last game was a 0-0 draw with my old club Bournemouth, now managed by my former teammate, John Benson. They had been relegated the previous season, the squad fatally weakened by a departing John Bond taking a number of players to Norwich City with him. The last game was against Lincoln: the site of my season-ending injury.

There was a vague notion that I was going to play in this game, as I was almost fit again – however, Musgrove thought this unwise. He was concerned that the Lincoln player who broke my leg earlier in the season might come unstuck, as our team may have taken the opportunity to get retribution on him. In the event, he was taken off in the second half, as some of my teammates were definitely keen to give him a hard time – we had a number of players who would have been quite capable of administering retribution. As you can imagine, we didn't stay for a beer with them after the game!

The summer was spent working on my fitness in preparation for the 1976/77 season. Having finished well in the Fourth Division the previous season, hopes were high. I began the campaign in the starting eleven, ironically against Bournemouth on 14th August in the League Cup, where I received a phenomenal reception from the fans. Playing in the unfamiliar number five shirt, we achieved a 0-0 draw at Dean Court. The crowd was fairly small –

2,687 – and the replay at Plainmoor attracted 3,439, where we managed to win 1-0. These two games proved to be very emotional occasions for me. To be up against one of my previous clubs, and players I used to play with, such as Keith Miller, was difficult. We went on to beat Burnley in the next round, before succumbing to Swansea in the third round.

All was not well for me, however. While mentally I felt good, following my injuries I didn't feel the same, physically speaking. Following my fourth game of the season against Bradford City on 18th September 1976, a defeat at home, I decided that I was no longer good enough to cope with football at this level. It was a heartbreaking decision to have to make at the age of 33, but I knew the edge had gone, and that there were moments during the match when I just couldn't push myself anymore. My physical and mental motivation just wasn't there.

It was frustrating, yes, but also very sad – my professional career had come to an end, and coming to terms with this took a lot of soul-searching. What was I going to do now: play lower down the league pyramid, become a coach or manager, or possibly find a job? After all, I had other qualifications, and had actually worked in schools coaching and teaching pupils. Perhaps a new career in teaching could be the answer, but where?

I was granted a testimonial game by Torquay, organised by manager Mike Green (Musgrove had departed by this point) and secretary Dave Easton in order to financially assist me. The plan was to play a game at Plainmoor against opposition that would attract a decent crowd. My first thought was Bournemouth, who I still had a good relationship with. My former club were keen, but then the idea came about: what about Torquay versus a combined team from the local area, like Exeter and Plymouth? This would undoubtedly be played in a competitive fashion, and attract more than just Torquay supporters.

I did not play in the match itself, but was actively involved in the pre- and post-match activities. A few drinks were shared after the game with the players, and the next day I drove back to Bournemouth. The event raised the princely sum of £430.55, less various expenses. That was it: I was no longer a professional footballer.

So having started my professional football career at Charlton in 1962, the curtain was brought down in June 1977 when my contract with Torquay ended, bringing to a close a fifteen-year career in full-time professional football with over 400 league appearances to my name.

The article for my testimonial programme was written by a good friend of mine, Dave Thomas, sportswriter for the Herald Express, Torquay's local paper. I feel that his words summed me up pretty well, some of which I've included here:

"He was a master tackler, a genuinely skilful player on the ball and read the game so well that he was seldom caught out on the turn. He affectionately referred to his left foot as 'The Scythe', but that was doing himself less than justice."

INTERLUDE

They don't make them like Dave Stocks anymore! Of course, that's a cliched thing for any reporter to say, and it's not completely true. There are a few, but they're few and far between these days.

The great shame of Dave's five years and 161 games at Plainmoor in the mid-1970s was that they coincided with a fallow time in the club's fortunes. The Gulls were never in danger of relegation, but various managers could never quite add the finishing touches to a team that included marvellous pros like Dave, Clint Boulton, Cliff Myers, Willie Brown and goalkeeper Mike Mahoney. All of them could have played at higher levels. Several did or, like Dave, had done. They should have won a promotion or two. They would have deserved it.

They didn't just play with 8/10 consistency every week, but they also taught the youngsters their trade in a way that hard-pressed managers often never did. Men you could go into the proverbial trenches with.

Dave – he was damn good at cricket and tennis too –

liked to call his left foot 'The Claw' (as well as the Scythe!). He was doing himself a gross injustice. It was more like a wand, and you don't get many of those at left-back or centre-back.

He was 33 when a second broken leg signalled the end as a full-time pro. Leg breaks nearly 50 years ago were not the routine injuries they are now. He'd done well to come back from the first one, and if it hadn't been for that second cruel intervention, he could have gone on for years, so clever and determined was he.

We've reminisced many times about those days, the marathon trips – Workington away with no M6? – hoping to get back to the English Riviera before the nightclubs shut. I know he came to rate his time at Torquay as among the happiest of his career. One thing's for sure: we were lucky to have him.

Dave Thomas
Sportswriter at the Herald Express

SEVEN

TIME FOR A REAL JOB!

Initially I didn't really miss playing, and I certainly didn't miss the training. It was the camaraderie and relationships with the other players, plus my relationship with the crowd, whose absence I felt most keenly. This may seem a little strange, but I always enjoyed playing in front of the spectators and giving one hundred per cent – I was value for money!

Although the training back then was not what it is now, and we had quite a bit of free time, I had filled my days with activities like coaching and teaching, which gave me a fairly active week. I have always needed a good structure in my life, and like to be busy, so it felt really strange to think that this part of my life was over, and that I needed to think about the future.

Back then, the kind of money a player earned in football wasn't what it is today. At the age of 33, I found myself in the position of having to consider what I was going to do for the rest of my life. After moving back to Bournemouth, I obviously needed to find work. I had obtained my Higher National Certificate in Structural Engineering before signing as a full-time professional for Charlton back in my London days. Also, throughout my football career, I had worked as a sports coach in schools during the afternoons after training, where I gained qualifications in coaching cricket, tennis and of course football. This resulted in me getting my Football Association full badge coaching licence at Lilleshall Football Coaching Centre, so I had a few options I could consider.

I was approached by Weymouth to become their manager around this point as well, and while I gave it serious consideration, I ultimately ended up turning them down. While on one hand I was keen to put my coaching badges to work, Weymouth were part-tim. I had it in my head that I would get a full-time job, and I probably wouldn't have been able to give management the attention it needed.

The world is your oyster, or so the saying goes, and I had numerous interviews around the Bournemouth area, and several in London and Brighton. Back in those days, qualifications were important, but not prized to the level they are nowadays, and I was anxious to make a decision on where my future lay. My contract with Torquay had expired at the end of June, and I had a reasonable sum in savings, plus the proceeds of my testimonial match, but I was keen to get on and see what the future held.

I did seriously consider staying in the professional game via coaching or management. I actually had an offer from Brighton, which I found strange, as I'd had no previous involvement with them during my career, although I had nearly signed for them from Charlton at one point. Ultimately, I turned down the offer – it was time for something completely different, and although football had given me a good career as a player, I felt it was time to leave the uncertainty and get a proper job.

I gained my FA coaching certificate at the age of 25 (I understand now that I was one of the youngest to do this at that point), so management was a viable option, but I didn't go down that route. There are no regrets here, however, as my subsequent career proved to be long and fulfilling on both a personal and financial level. Having spent a lot of time throughout my career coaching at local schools, I even considered becoming a full-time teacher at one point, with Castle Court offering me a position.

After many weeks of deliberation and sleepless nights, I made my decision. It would have been easy to take the simple route and start teaching and coaching in schools – it was a nice way of earning a living, and the holidays were good too. However, I felt that I needed more of a challenge, as well as the prospect of higher earnings later on.

My mother's earlier insistence that I kept up my studies and gained qualifications proved to be most valuable. Three days after my testimonial, I had an interview with Hambro Life, an insurance and investment company based in Bournemouth, to work as a financial adviser. Thus commenced what was to prove to be a very successful and fulfilling 41-year career in financial services.

-

My football days were not over, however. I was keen to keep my fitness levels up, and I carried on playing locally as an amateur. As a recently retired professional footballer, there were plenty of very accommodating teams to choose from, and I ended up playing on Saturday and Sunday mornings, as well as Wednesday afternoons.

My programme of events was as follows: playing for Parley Sports, and later Wimborne Town, on Saturday; in the Dorset Combination league on Sundays for Grange Sports, and on Wednesday afternoons for various teams. These match days provided something of an obvious contrast to the league games I had been used to, the most challenging aspect of which were the pitches. Replacing the stadiums I had been used to were local parks like King's Park, Kinson Recreation Ground and Slades Farm (not an actual farm, I hasten to add, but a field with several pitches, which managed to somehow be windswept even in the summer). The crowds were somewhat different too – from the 54,000 or so at Anfield or Stamford Bridge, we just had the proverbial one man and his dog!

My job with Hambro was fairly flexible in terms of hours. The way it was structured meant that I was essentially self-employed, so I was able to tailor my week so I could play Wednesday afternoon league football. Over the course of my years in this league, the team bore several different monikers, most notably Gran Moda, although it took its name from anyone who was prepared to sponsor us. These included Grange Hotel, Armadillo Aces, Hambro

Life (of course), G&Ts and Lorenzo Restaurant (the eponymous Lorenzo, who also owned La Lupa restaurant in Poole, played for us). At one point we were even known as 'The Police' – the real deal, not the band – even though we, somewhat bizarrely, did have a connection to the band: one of our players was Rickie Summers, the brother of guitarist Andy. On the odd occasion, Andy would drop by and watch, or even come on as a substitute (he was a much better musician than he was a footballer!). Our opposition included the Marines (who lived up to their reputation; you did not want to mess with them) and several hotels and restaurants, with their players consisting of waiters or bar staff. So long as they were back to serve dinner after the match, all was well.

Our team was made up of anyone who could get the time off work, so most of them tended to be business owners, service personnel or employees of the business owners, either playing or sponsoring the team. There were also a number of other Hambro Life people, as the role of financial adviser seemed to attract ex-professional footballers, with former Bournemouth players Terry Shanahan and Peter Johnson among their number. Another ex-pro involved was Twiggy Partridge, who had spent time at Southampton and Blackpool. He was pretty eccentric – I remember him playing one game at Fernheath in plimsolls, although that didn't stop him putting away a last-minute penalty. His speciality was flicking a coin up in the air, catching it on his foot, then flicking it back up into the air and into his trouser pocket.

The opposition players were always surprised to see me,

and questioned why I would choose to play at this level. To be honest, I just enjoyed the camaraderie and the chance to play with my mates. It also meant I got the chance to play out of position in midfield instead of defence, but mostly it was great for my fitness, and the games were generally quite friendly. On the odd occasion, however, there would be a match that wasn't played in such an amicable fashion. You would sometimes get someone looking to make a name for themselves who had recognised me from my professional playing days, decided I was fair pickings, and subsequently tried to take me out. Fortunately, this only happened occasionally, and was not really a problem. I wasn't the only ex-pro in the league, and most were just happy to be pitting themselves against them. Plus, having played against some very physical opponents during my career, I was more than capable of taking care of myself.

At weekends, I would play for Parley in the Dorset Combination League. This was a great deal more competitive than the other teams I played for, but we were the beneficiary of several other ex-professionals in our line-up, in addition to myself, meaning that we won most games. Standing out was Steve Webb, who spent some time at Bournemouth as a youngster. Shanahan in particular scored an immense amount, putting away some 40-50 goals a season. Parley did pay some of their players, although not me, and I wasn't too fussed about this. My take was that I really only wanted to turn up and play on Saturdays at a reasonable standard and in a ground with decent facilities, so Parley was perfect for me. They had a nice pitch with a great clubhouse and, most of all, good people.

Things got a little more interesting when we played away at the likes of Shaftesbury, Blandford, Sturminster Newton, Gillingham and Portland. The problem was that the opposition were a little jealous of Parley, as we were a town team, and as this was a Dorset league, most of the teams were from local villages. The home matches at Parley Cross were generally peaceful affairs that we would win comfortably – it was the away trips that were not so comfortable. Gillingham in particular stood out – there was an electric fence around the pitch to keep the crowds back.

It was a big day in some of the villages when Parley hit town, and to say that some of the games were physical would have been an understatement. As a team with a sprinkling of ex-pros, we knew how to take care of ourselves, but the opposition were mainly made up of local farm workers, labourers and the odd mechanic, so their talents on the pitch were rather agricultural! Although the crowds were low in numbers, they were fairly intimidating to say the least, something that was especially the case during ties at Portland.

There was apparently some history between the two clubs; to some involved, this was war, not a football match. Some of their players were residents of the nearby prison, and were let out to play for the team on Saturday afternoons. The prison was previously a military fort, having been built in the mid-19th century as a garrison home for the nearby Portland naval base. It became a category C prison in 1949, and was at this time being used as a centre for young offenders. We got changed in the same facilities as them, which was a bit worrying, although they were very friendly during my time playing against them. A draw was always a good result, as this kept both sides happy, so to leave unscathed with a 1-1 draw suited us.

The crowd were unsurprisingly hostile, but the groundsman, a guy named Percy, was something else. He would offer non-stop abuse as soon as you left the dressing room, and would keep going right up until the end of the match. But that wasn't all; the bath at Portland was placed under the wooden floorboards. At the game's end, if it was your first time at Portland, you would be unaware that you had to stop immediately upon entering the dressing room, as within one step was this bath filled with scalding-hot water (compliments of Percy, naturally).

I also played on Sunday mornings. It was early days for Sunday league football, but I was better known by the opposition, as this was a Bournemouth league. There were no real issues from the opposition though, and as with the Saturday fixtures, most were happy to play it fair. We had a mixture of talent (if that's what you would call it!), with a number of the side having played at a reasonable level. The background of the players varied from youngsters who were physically fit and could do the legwork, but lacked real skill, to more mature players like myself. The combination of youth and wisdom made for a reasonable starting XI.

The main factor preventing our rise to greatness was the 10.30am Sunday morning kick-off time, as most of the team would have been out the night before, which proved a nightmare for the manager in his attempts to put together a full team before kick-off. This combination of factors didn't always make for a feast of football, but they had the potential to be as memorable as any I participated in during my professional career.

-

One match that stands out in my memory was at King's Park in Boscombe – not the best of venues, but the pitch was close to Dean Court. The dressing room was slowly – too slowly – filling up by 10am, with 30 minutes until kick-off. At that point we had just seven players, with the conversations centring on the antics during the previous night out on the town from the youngsters. Trying to bring the focus onto the game was not easy – for a start, no one was keen to take on the role of goalkeeper; they all wanted to play on the pitch, score the goals and get the glory, with comments such as, "It's football, not handball, why would we want to go in goal?"

With minutes to spare, our goalkeeper Sergio arrived, mumbling something in Spanish by way of apology. He was a relatively new signing, working at a local Italian restaurant owned by Tony Deangelis, our main sponsor, and claimed to have once played for the Real Madrid junior side. We were not sure of his credentials, but he looked the part, being tall and athletic, and more than a bit theatrical between the posts. The rest of the team were now arriving – some looked in reasonably good condition, others less so. Most would have played for another team on the day before like me, so there would have been a few knocks that needed to be allowed for.

By 10.30 it was kick-off time, and we still only had ten men. Fortunately, the opposition were in the same situation. Our missing player was Tony Sword – often known as Swordy – a local businessman who was quite often late. We couldn't drop him, as his company, G&T, also sponsored the side. Plus, he wasn't a bad player when he showed up. As the opposition's eleventh player arrived, we undertook a possession-based approach. Ten minutes in, it was still 0-0. The word on the absence of Tony was that he was last seen at about 4am getting into a taxi heading to a casino in Bournemouth, so the chances of him showing up were slim.

20 minutes in, with the score still at 0-0, it started to rain. Our opponents weren't of the best quality, even with a full side, and our team was starting to sober up, with the tackles starting to bite. At this point, Swordy finally arrived, and we were back up to eleven players. It was developing into a good match, but the rain was now chucking it down, and it was getting cold. Moreover, I found myself constantly getting kicked by this young, mouthy, overweight opposition player, who was obviously intent on doing some damage to me. After one foul too many, I informed him that if he did that one more time then I would have to hurt him, and as I used to do that for a living (play football, not hurt people!), I would probably succeed! Fortunately, one of their players knew who I was, and confirmed to him that he should stop doing it, as he would certainly get hurt, and that I was quite knowledgeable about the darker side of football. It's amazing what a reputation I had acquired, and how useful it was!

Halfway through the second half, we were winning 2-0 thanks to a couple of bits of magic from Angelo Paperella, a waiter from Tony's restaurant. He had apparently been on Juventus's books prior to coming to the UK, and played in Italy's Serie C until a broken leg put paid to his professional career. Despite being a bit volatile, he was a good player. From midfield I was able to provide passes to him, and we gelled immediately – it was like the old days at Bournemouth, feeding balls up to Ted MacDougall and Phil Boyer. It lifted my spirits on these cold, wet Sunday mornings. I enjoyed playing at this level, even though some of the players were obviously amateurs. Being an ex pro, you are able to see the passes you want to make, and if you can receive a ball early from a teammate, that gives you more time on the ball and makes it possible to lift the overall standard of the game.

Inevitably though, this couldn't go on forever. Having retired from the professional game, eventually the time comes when you ask yourself if it is time to grow up and retire completely from playing. For me, this came about at the age of 44 – time waits for no man, and the legs were no longer working as well as they used to. Having played for Parley for a number of years, I turned out for Wimborne Town for a while before finally hanging up my boots. It was a strange feeling, having played from the age of ten in London for my school and district, to peaking – if that's the right expression – with the career highlight of an FA Cup third-round tie in front of a crowd of 24,388 at Dean Court. Try picturing that now!

-

Even after I had retired, there was still time for me to face off against one of the greatest players of all time. It took place in the fairly inauspicious surroundings of Victoria Park, home of Bournemouth Poppies, where I was playing in a charity match involving a number of former players – Harry Redknapp might have been there, along with the likes of Andy Jones, John Williams and some other former pros. By my understanding, the organisers had invited a lot of players to participate, hoping that there would be enough for 11 on each side should some of them fail to show up. In the event, they needn't have worried, as virtually everyone they invited made an appearance. Among their number – amazingly – was George Best himself. He had recently played a number of games for Bournemouth, and while he wasn't the same player by that point, shades of his ability remained.

Why he was so good is hard to describe – he just *did* things. One moment he was in front of you, and the next he went past you like you weren't there. You'd move in, and then he was gone. I remember going in for a tackle – I went left, he went right, and with that he nutmegged me. I recall telling him that I'd prefer he didn't do that again, and he just smiled and did it again. He may have been long past his prime, but the ability was still there.

In total, my professional career saw me play 442 league games with four teams: Charlton, Gillingham, Bournemouth and finally Torquay. It would have been nice to have made it to the 500 mark, but the two broken legs during my Plainmoor stint put paid to that. Even so, it's not a bad total!

INTERLUDE

*The first time I saw Dave play was in 1968, shortly before
the Liverpool game at Dean Court. I remember going to the
Bury game in bitterly cold rain, with the Cherries winning
1-0. Dave obviously didn't do anything of note, so I can't say
whether he played well or not – he didn't launch anybody,
at least!*

*Liverpool had all their great players of that time – Roger
Hunt, Ian St John, Emlyn Hughes, etc – but the two standouts
were Ian Callaghan and Peter Thompson. Thompson in
particular was incredibly quick. I was later to learn from
Dave that he and Terry Gulliver had spent a considerable
amount of time during the week working out their strategy
of Dave marking Thompson and Gully marking Callaghan.
However, when they kicked off, Callaghan had switched to
Dave's side of the pitch and Thompson to Gully's side, much
to their bemusement!*

*I next came across Dave playing for Bournemouth in
a friendly at Sturminster Marshall, my hometown. All my
schoolmates waited at the changing rooms for autographs*

after the game. *The autograph books and newspaper clippings were taken into the changing rooms, and when they were returned, Dave had signed five of mine, so in my eyes he was a legend! It sounds odd to say, but because he had signed all those photos, when I went to watch a number of evening games against the likes of Scunthorpe (Kevin Keegan played) and Workington (the night John Meredith broke his leg horribly), I would take more of an interest in Dave. Seeing him close up playing and supporting Tony Scott down the left wing, I got to see that despite him being rather aggressive towards opposing wingers, he also had quite a cultured left foot.*

Shortly after that, I joined Bournemouth as a youngster. As part of our job, myself and the other apprentices had to clean the first team's boots. As you can imagine, there was normally a rush for Ted and Phil's, so I would often get the boots belonging to those that were not deemed to be star players – like Dave. More on this later! It was during this time that I got to know Dave personally, in somewhat unlikely circumstances. After training one morning I had a painful blister on my foot and was told by Trevor Hartley to see the trainer, Arthur Cunliffe. Arthur was very much of the old school, with the old baggy tracksuit bottoms tucked into his rolled-down socks – a real bucket-and-sponge trainer! Dave was being treated for an injury himself at the time, and we got on.

My other memory of Dave at Bournemouth was one morning at the training ground of Bournemouth Electric. On numerous occasions there would be first team versus reserves matches (the reserves' manager, John Kirk, treated these events like a local derby), with this one taking place on a Thursday morning. As some of the first teamers had already learnt their fate for Saturday's match, this game attracted a high degree of physicality, particularly for those who wanted their starting spot back. I was playing on the left wing facing Gully, and my fellow youth player, Stevie Jeapes, was on the right facing Dave. Jeapes was a flying winger, and was trying to take Dave on. Well, Dave wasn't going to have any of that, and sure enough, Jeapsey was launched off the pitch again and again! After another launching, Jeapsey was screaming to swap wings. I remember looking at Gully, and he had that smile as if to say, "You don't want to be going over there!" It was incredible that with a big game less than 48 hours away, lumps were being kicked out of each other!

I next met up with Dave when he had finished playing at Torquay and we played for Gran Moda in the Bournemouth Sunday League. Gran Moda, a clothing outfitters, was owned by Tony Deangelis, who also owned the La Lupa restaurant chain. It was quite a strange setup compared to other teams, as each week you would turn up and see which ex professionals would be in the changing room – Dennis Walker (who played with George Best in the 1964 Youth Cup Final for Manchester United, and went on to play for York and Cambridge), Bob Walker and Les Parodi all made appearances – as well as a number of top Dorset players, like Barrie Collie, Bobby Way and Terry Mitchell. The majority of the rest of the team would be made up of Italian La Lupa employees, such as Angelo Paperella, formerly of Serie C, whose career in professional football had ended following a broken leg. Angelo was playing with me for Blandford, so I brought him to play for Moda, where he was treated like a hero by the rest of the Italian contingent. Team talks were in English and Italian!

Sunday League football was a strange environment, as players would turn up with 25 minutes to go until kick-off. The chat would be, "Has anybody seen Gareth?" "Out of his mind outside some Bournemouth nightclub at 2:30 this morning!" I played next to Dave in midfield and having had a hard game on Saturday, I was content to just give the ball to Dave and let him do the creative bit.

At this time, Dave was playing for Parley in the Dorset Combination League, and I was at Blandford. We had a few encounters, but the one I remember most was in the Dorset Combination Cup Final at Bournemouth Water Company's ground. We were winning 3-1 with a few minutes to go when I went on a jinking run past two or three players. I distinctly recall going past the halfway line after going past another player when everything in my mind slowed down. I couldn't hear the crowd shouting; just silence. It was at this moment I realised I was about to be launched by Dave. I thought I did quite well, as I was off the ground before he connected! Wiping the mud from my face, I looked at him, and he smiled and said, "Webby, you've won, so don't take the piss!"

We lost touch after that until we met at Castle Court School at a parents' evening after my daughters, Sarah and Laura, had joined. He very quickly introduced me to the deputy head, saying, "Webby is a cricketer, get him in the parents' team!" We continued our friendship at school *functions at Castle Court and later Clayesmore School in Iwerne Minster, during parent cricket matches against other schools, and while us and our wives, Janet and Debbie, chauffeured them around various golf clubs. Over this time, our families have remained close. On my 50th birthday, our friends and families went down to Okehampton in Devon to stay for a few days in this large farm cottage. One evening, Dave gave me a large birthday present. When I opened it, it was filled with various shoe polishes and brushes. He said "Now, clean them properly!"*

On the subject of holidays, we all went down to Torquay a couple of years ago. While we were there, we went to Plainmoor on the off chance that we could take a look at the ground. While peering through the gates, the young assistant groundsman came over and enquired what we were doing there. Rather taken aback, David said humbly that he had played for Torquay and was just having a look around. With that, there was a shout of "Stocksy, what the f*** are you doing here?" The old groundsman had appeared, and respect to the former captain was given by all. While reminiscing, Dave Thomas, who had reported on Torquay's games for decades, was brought in. An hour or so, we left with Dave's stature as a professional footballer held high. Once a legend, always a legend!

Steve Webb

EIGHT

IT'S NOT ALL ABOUT FOOTBALL!

This book has mainly covered my football days, but my love of sport was not limited to this. As I touched upon earlier, cricket also played a big part in my life, starting in the streets of south London with a bit of wood as a bat, continuing right up to playing for Dorset over 50s.

In my school days, during the summer my mates and I would travel to Brockwell Park near Brixton and play five-day test matches, trying to emulate our heroes, such as Alec Bedser and Peter May. At weekends during term time, we would play all-day matches at Norwood Park. My cricketing skills were, in my opinion, better than my footballing ones. Having been selected to represent London schoolboys for both cricket and football, my sporting career could have gone either way.

When I joined Charlton as a semi-professional and

was working at Harvey's doing my HNC, I played cricket for Harvey's in some local friendlies, as there weren't any leagues back then. Charlton also had a cricket team that played in a few friendlies, as some of their members, like Stuart Leary and Fred Lucas, were also county cricketers playing for Kent. Supplemented by the club's South African contingent, we had a formidable team. For my part, I was asked to play for the side to make up the numbers and do the fielding. There weren't many games, and they only took place after the football season had finished.

I was never one for being idle, and because the training schedule was reasonably light and the season quite short, I found time alongside studying for my coaching certificate for some more leisurely activities like tennis and golf. Accompanied by Keith Peacock, I endeavoured to master these. Inevitably, being a competitive sportsman, even these sports would later become more than just leisure activities. I even got my tennis coaching certificate during this time, which came in handy during my time working at the local schools.

As there wasn't much in the way of youth or even amateur leagues back when I was young, coaching programs were limited, unlike today. It was only when I joined Harvey's that my cricketing skills really developed. I have a feeling that Peter Croker – who was involved in getting me my contract at Charlton, as well as the job at Harvey's – had an inkling that I might be a useful member of the cricket team too. The line-up was exceptional, possessing a number of high-quality players, such as Leon Hellmuth, Mike Golder and John Aitchison, who all had county links with Kent. Although I initially joined as a fielder, it wasn't long before my batting and bowling skills were noticed. Under my teammates' guidance, I improved enough to be included.

We played on both Saturdays and Sundays, and it proved to be a perfect education in cricket from a group of talented and friendly teammates, playing at many picturesque grounds around the suburbs of South London and the county of Kent. As there was little money in the sport professionally back then, it was obvious that my involvement was only going to be for leisure. However, I still held a great passion for it, so I was happy to undertake the travelling needed to get from Dulwich to Blackheath both days of the weekend, even though I had done this journey all week. If we played away in Kent then that meant a longer journey, with matches starting at 2.30pm and finishing about 7-8pm on a Saturday, and all-day games on a Sunday starting at 11.30am. The biggest negative was travelling all the way to the ground only to be told it was rained off. No mobile phones – or landlines, for that matter – existed to let you know not to bother travelling. I continued to play for Harvey's even when I had signed as a full time professional for Charlton and no longer worked for them, an arrangement that remained in place until I was sold to Gillingham. I carried on playing cricket for a local side, but ultimately only took part in a few games, since I was only there for a season.

-

When I joined Bournemouth in June 1966, I took on a part-time summer job with Kennedy's, a local builders' merchants. This came about as other players had already been working at Kennedy's during the close season and put me forward (you probably wouldn't get too many professional footballers taking on summer jobs nowadays!). The only condition was that I agreed to play cricket for them, as they were well known on the local business cricket circuit and were keen to improve their kudos, even though the matches were supposed to be friendlies! Sadly, this arrangement only lasted two summers, as the cricket team folded at the end of summer 1967. Perhaps not uncoincidentally, my part-time job ended with it.

I wasn't left inactive on the cricket front for too long, though – Michael Wheeler introduced me to Donald Scott, the headmaster at Castle Court School, and I started coaching with them which helped with replacement part-time earnings. Having played a few matches for Kennedy's, my name was now known in the local cricket arena. In the summer of 1968, I was approached by Tony Street, who worked in local government and played for Moordown Cricket Club, a local side in the first division of the Bournemouth league. Kennedy's used to play in the same league as Moordown, which was how Tony spotted me. My playing relationship with Moordown would last for over 30 years, bar a few years in Torquay, where I turned out for Barton Cricket Club.

I would continue playing cricket in the close season throughout my professional football career. When I look back at how it was possible to be on a full-time contract, but still able to do so much in the way of other sports and activities, it seems unbelievable – it certainly wouldn't happen now. I think being a sportsman was in my blood, and I was always going to play one sport or another whenever possible.

When my professional footballing career came to an end in 1977 and I returned to Bournemouth to start a proper job, I was keen to keep playing sport. I rekindled my connection with Moordown and played for them until the late 1990s, when the club folded. Moordown was highly regarded in the Bournemouth area, attracting a host of talented players. We even encouraged some ex-professional footballers to join the ranks, including the likes of Steve Gritt, Andy Jones and Keith Clapham.

Having crafted my cricketing skills under the guidance of some great players back in the 1960s, I was able to fine-tune these while playing for Moordown and became a keystone of the side, eventually captaining it for several seasons. My talent was mainly with the ball rather than the bat, but the record books show I wasn't too shabby at either. I was an unusual combination of left arm round the wicket swing bowler and a right-handed batsman, batting at 3 or 4, but I was only part of the team; I played with and against some of the most talented amateur cricketers in the area. Moordown regularly finished around the top of the league, thanks to the likes of Martin Page, the Rattue brothers, Mickey Roy, Brian Gosby, Geoff Cox and Pete Challen, to name a few. With Tony Street as our captain, we were the team that everyone wanted to beat.

They also had an amazing youth setup run by Bert

Biles, who would regularly produce youngsters with incredible talent. These included Owen Parkin, who went on to play county cricket for Glamorgan. Moordown had a first team playing in the Bournemouth League Division One, as well as a second team in Division Five. Eventually, they entered the Dorset League that played on Sundays, with these two teams used to blood the younger players. The Sunday matches were a bit more social, with wives, girlfriends and family often coming along to support at lovely local villages such as Shroton, Milton Abbas, Burley and Minstead.

When I turned 50 in 1993, I was selected to play for Dorset over 50s. With Dorset being a minor county, its success was limited, but during my time playing for them we did manage to make it to the National League finals, playing against Lancashire. We also took on other teams, such as Devon, Cornwall, Hampshire and even Jersey, so we got to travel to some amazing grounds, which provided some great experiences.

There were also some memorable times on the work side, with our financial consultancy business supporting various corporate cricket days. There was one particular event that we sponsored for several years, which was the cricket week in Wimborne, played at the old ground in the middle of the town. The event was organised by the club, with matches against touring sides and other local business teams. On one of the days, current players from Hampshire were invited to play, including the likes of Robin and Chris Smith, Malcolm Marshall and Mark Nicholas. Local businesses would enter a team for this day, and would be allocated a Hampshire player for their team. We entered a team for several years on the trot and were given Mark Nicholas and Chris Smith on a couple of those. As this was 'my' team, I would assume the role of captain, which was not an issue with Chris Smith – he was a real team player and took the event in the spirit of what it was: a fun, friendly tournament. Mark Nicholas, on the other hand, wasn't so happy with playing second fiddle to me, a mere local player. There was a lot of banter throughout the day, and even with two captains with opposing opinions we managed to win the tournament. It was at this event that I also had the pleasure (if you can call it that) of facing the bowling of the master himself, Malcolm Marshall. He did slow it down a bit for my benefit, but the ball still passed my bat at lightning speed!

I continued to play for the over 50s after my time with Moordown and local league cricket finished, but not for many seasons. I found it hard to just pick up the bat or turn my arm over to bowl without the regular practice of weekly league matches. I think it was around the turn of the millennium that I eventually hung up my bat and gloves. After this, I took up the golf clubs again, and started on the next journey of my sporting endeavours.

Dorset over 50s is still running, and I occasionally manage to watch a few of their matches. There are still a few faces from my cricketing time that are actively involved, whether playing or umpiring. They also now have tours abroad, which wasn't something that happened when I was playing, and I was fortunate enough to go with them in 2021 to Barbados. Sadly, no cricket was played due to Covid restrictions, but a great holiday was had by all.

It was nice to spend time and reminisce about playing in the team, especially with my good friend Steve Webb, who if you recall I was first connected with during my time at Bournemouth, as he was one of the juniors who used to clean my boots – a fact that he is reminded of regularly!

Also, there was a good friend, Richard Turner, who was a formidable player for Witchampton, another local cricket team. He was there in the capacity as umpire, as his playing days were over, but he and I chatted at length about our days when we would do battle. It was during these conversations that I started to realise the shadows I must have created, based on his recollections of his team waiting in anticipation for the team sheet to see if I was due to play. I didn't realise that I was the hot topic of conversation!

-

Although I had hung up my bat and gloves on the competitive cricket arena, it would not be the end of my time playing. When our sons, Oliver and Alex, were born, Debra and I took a trip along to Castle Court to discuss putting their names down for places in their nursery and prep school. What we didn't know was that word had got around that I was coming to the school, and a few of the teachers – in particular the director of sport, Steve Ives – were keen to meet me. It turned out that he was a pupil when I was coaching there during my time at

Bournemouth and Torquay. Castle Court had a teacher/parent cricket team, called the 'Crustacens', and as an ex-teacher and now parent, they were keen for me to join the team. How could I refuse? The matches were supposed to be friendlies against other local prep and secondary schools, such as Dumpton, Bryanston and Canford, but there was a fierce rivalry between the schools – nothing 'friendly' about them!

After being a parent at Castle Court for a few years, a suggestion was made that a parent/teacher football team should be set up too. By this time I was well past being a player, so happily took on the manager role – a decision that I at times regretted, especially when I was berated by a keen parent or teacher as to why I had taken them off. As the majority of the players didn't have the stamina to play for a full 90 minutes, we had rolling subs. Not only did this give some a much-needed rest, it also meant we could give more an opportunity to play.

We were fortunate to have some talented players, who although were no longer in their prime, could still display their skills on the pitch. The hardest to manage was an Icelandic international and former Premier League player. Hermann Hreiðarsson – 89 caps for Iceland, and veteran of the top level for Portsmouth, Charlton, Ipswich and others – and his wife Ragna, who also represented Iceland for the women's team – were parents at the school. Ragna was a great team player and much easier to manage than Hermann – he, on the other hand, used his size to try to influence my decision as to how long I could keep him on the pitch!

I have often been asked why I didn't go into management when my playing career ended, and to be honest, at times I have asked myself that question. I think it could have been a possibility, but the offer of a job in the financial sector and away from football was a breath of fresh air, and a much-needed change at the time. If you asked me now, having managed the Castle Court Casuals, my answer would be that I'm pleased with the route I took!

Golf is the sport that has been my passion for the last 30 years. I can't say that I have the same ability as I did in cricket and football – I never managed to get to a single-figure handicap, only reaching 11 before heading back the other way. However, I have still been able to enjoy it with friends and my family. Both my sons took it up at a young age, have both represented the county, and are now scratch golfers. It has made me really proud to see them achieve success, although it's embarrassing when I have to take two shots for every one they take!

Golf has been a great sport to play, from my early days at Charlton as a leisure activity with Keith, to playing fairly competitively when I stopped playing cricket 30 years ago. I could never see life without me playing some form of sport, but with the injuries sustained during my footballing days, I have had to adapt!

NINE

LEGACY

As I sit at my desk, trying to recall my sporting history, surrounded by football programmes, newspaper cuttings, photographs and other autobiographies penned by sporting legends and not-so legends, I can take the time to reflect on how sport has shaped my life. My experiences have been gathered over many years, and now at nearly 80 years of age, it is 60 years of experiences that I reflect on. Although I am unable to play sport to the same level that I used to, I still have many sporting interests, mainly consisting of watching and playing the odd game of tennis and golf.

It is nice that here in Bournemouth I still get recognised for my footballing exploits, either because of how I look (which hasn't changed much) or my name. Today, Bournemouth has a higher profile thanks to its recent time spent in the Premier League, although the older supporters still remember the good old days! Funnily enough, I still get asked for my signature – a couple of times, autograph hunters have called into my old office in Westbourne, and I have even had some call in at my home. Charlton, who have a great ex-players setup, have invited me up to watch a few matches, and people in the supporters bar love to come over and chat about players and teams from the '60s and '70s.

The difference in the game from when I played compared to nowadays couldn't be more pronounced – training, coaching, the pace of the game and the physical and mental demands put on the players have become so different that it would be pointless to make comparisons. In this data-driven landscape, any information on the opposition is ready to hand: opposition tactics at goal kicks, corners and free kicks are analysed and laid bare, as are the individual strengths and weaknesses of key players.

Having watched a number of Bournemouth matches in the Premier League, it's clear that the standard of opposition at the top level is incredible – in some cases among the best in the world. I played with and against many international stars, but the standard of talent and fitness in the highest division today is far superior. The day-to-day training routines are far more structured and measured, with focus placed on fitness, diet and mental strength in order to achieve maximum returns from the players. They are coached and trained specifically with their positions on the pitch in mind, and this has resulted in a marked improvement. When you consider that training back in the day involved running around the pitch, followed by a small-sided game on the tarmac by the side of the stand, things were definitely more relaxed. There were less 'behind closed doors' matches too – practice matches were 'first team versus reserves' affairs, with the reserves supplemented by youth teamers. As Steve Webb mentioned in his chapter, it wasn't always fun for the youngsters!

The actual technique of players is generally better too, even with the defenders. The footballs used now are much lighter, and the playing surfaces are far better – some of the ones I played on amounted to little more than waterlogged fields. I can vividly remember some northern grounds in particular where the weather tended to be noticeably worse than it was in the south. When receiving the ball, you had to flick the ball up with one foot and volley it with the other in order to get anywhere. It was almost impossible to pass the ball properly due to the poor condition of the pitch. It was important to keep the ball up in the air, and when a cross was made to the attackers, hopefully they could take a shot at goal or head it in. This was probably the most effective technique back then, but with today's superior pitches, a more structured approach can be applied, resulting in a lot more passing of the ball. As a result, the game is much better to watch for the purist.

There are fewer physical confrontations today, believe it or not, which for me at least make the games less exciting! While less fighting can't be seen as a bad thing, it does seem to have come hand in hand with an increased amount of play-acting and attempts to get players sent off, which I have never liked. Believe it or not, the standard of refereeing has improved, with fewer mistakes and bias. In my opinion, referees today often have their work cut out with the kind of things they have to deal with.

There is also a lot of discussion nowadays about the impact of heading the ball and a possible link with dementia. I can see how my generation of players could have been impacted, as not only was the ball a heavy leather one, it was often quite wet and muddy, making it even heavier and potentially more dangerous.

Diet certainly wasn't a big consideration then either – we could basically eat what we wanted during the week. The pre-match meal wasn't exactly focused on marginal gains either – sometimes it was steak. After the match, we would all have a beer, which was a big part of the game back then. The players joined the supporters in the public bar at home matches, and you would quite regularly see players put away a pint or four. On occasions, at away matches we would have a few in the supporters' bar before the trip home, but only if we won – if not then it was straight back on the coach with a coke and sandwiches. If it was a win, we could stop off on route for a couple of beers and a meal in a restaurant. This was not always a good idea if the coach trip was long, as this would result in many toilet breaks. If the manager wasn't in a good mood then the stops would be limited and alternative arrangements would have to be devised. I won't go into detail; just use your imagination!

Sometimes it was not just the manager that was keen to get back down south in a hurry. The players would encourage the coach driver to put his foot down so they could get back before closing time, or at least early enough for them to go to the clubs in town. We had a regular coach driver when I was at Torquay, and he would do his best to get us back before closing. In fact, once he had dropped off the coach, he would join us. Alcohol was definitely part of the culture back then.

One thing I've taken from my experiences as a footballer into my career in finance is communication. Back then, players at my level didn't have a lot of media duties, but there was still a lot of meeting and speaking to people – supporters, reporters, not to mention the process of negotiating your own contract. There were no agents; you would sit in the boardroom with the directors and negotiate your contract. I had a reasonable grounding in this: my education was as good as it could have been, and I was fortunate to go to school in Dulwich, one of the nicest areas in London. It was a very disciplined school, and you either had to be reasonably bright to get in, or good at sport – preferably both.

-

So how would I have coped with the game as it's played today? This is a question that I get asked a lot by supporters. You would expect me to say that I would be fine, and I genuinely think I would be, as it would have suited my style of play. I was fortunate to be physically strong and a comfortable runner. I was happy with physical challenges, and found carrying the ball fairly easy – it was never a struggle for me to make a number of short or long runs up and down the flank.

During my playing days I was an attacking full-back, happy to overlap my team's winger when he was in possession of the ball and provide crosses into the penalty area for our forwards to attack. Crucially, I was then able to sprint back to my defensive position once I had delivered the ball. During my time at Bournemouth, I had two left wingers I regularly partnered with: John Meredith and Tony Scott. John in particular was perfect for me, and we produced some great moves. Unfortunately, a broken leg put paid to his career at Bournemouth. John and I had a great understanding, making it perfect for me to go on the outside past him when he had the ball, and the same for him when I had the ball. This would all be done in the opponents' half, confusing them as they would not know who was crossing the ball, with Ted and Phil waiting to pounce when the cross came in.

Tony was a little different; he was an exceptional crosser of the ball. He would use me as a decoy when he had the ball, cutting inside and crossing or shooting. He and I were particularly effective at Bournemouth, as Ted MacDougall thrived on the crosses in the box that helped make him one of the most prolific goalscorers in the late '60s and early '70s.

I still follow the clubs I played for and watch their fortunes ebb and flow. Not only has the playing style changed, but also the grounds. Back then, most of them consisted primarily of standing terraces. I recall the legendary terracing at Charlton with fond memories, except for when we were made to run up and down them during training. I probably hold the softest spot for

Bournemouth, as that was the club I played for the longest. Having stayed living locally, I have enjoyed watching their trials, tribulations and success. My time under Freddie Cox was enjoyable – however, even though it was quite short, playing under John Bond probably taught me the most about the game. I had an excellent relationship with the crowd, and as a spectator, it was great to witness the most successful period in the club's history under the management of Eddie Howe.

My last port of call on the professional ladder – even if it was on the way down – at Torquay, was great. They were a very friendly and welcoming club for both players and supporters. They were very accommodating with my travel arrangements, as it was always my intention to return to Bournemouth. I think the directors at Torquay were disappointed that I didn't stay down there in a coaching or management capacity – indeed, they made several offers in an attempt to persuade me to do so.

On a recent trip down to Torquay, I was able to take a literal trip down memory lane and visit the ground. Although the pandemic was a recent memory, the welcome we got from the groundsmen that had been preparing the ground for an evening match was just as warm as it was when I was a player. We were able to spend time (socially distanced, of course) reminiscing about the old days, as well as catching up on how the club is getting on now.

Torquay have had some low points in recent years, at one point dropping to the Conference South, but things look to be picking up now, with a great manager at the time of writing in Gary Johnson. The lads were telling us that with his connections, he has been able to negotiate the arrival of some promising youngsters on loan. While they are still one promotion away from a return to the Football League, hopefully this won't remain the case for too much longer.

The club's willingness and overriding support for these players to move to Torquay, even if only temporarily, is still evident today, as the club owns a sizable property next to the ground that houses up to eight players. It is refreshing to see that even with all the problems facing clubs at grassroots level, they still go the extra mile to look after their players and supporters.

-

The managerial side of football is hugely important. Nowadays, managers often benefit from a team of support staff, especially at the highest level. Back when I was playing, the coaching team was normally comprised solely of the manager, possibly accompanied by an assistant and a trainer. The trainer would be responsible for matchday treatment for players – these were the days of the magic sponge, capable of curing many ailments, ranging from bruises and strains to full-blown concussion. There were no substitutes in those days (until 1965 when my best mate, Charlton's Keith Peacock, made history by becoming the Football League's first ever substitute), and even then there was only one allowed per team). If you got injured, you carried on in your position as best you could – anything fairly serious and you were put on the wing.

The treatment for injuries was interesting, to say the least, as in most cases the trainer was not qualified to the level they are today – it was almost the case that you administered your own treatment. I injured my wrist in one match, and was told to carry on, the reasoning being, "You use your feet, don't you?" Later on in life, I had to have surgery on my wrist due to carpal tunnel, and the surgeon asked if I realised that I had at some point broken my hand. I didn't, as I hadn't had it looked at after the match; I just got it strapped up and assumed it was a sprain!

The style of management varied between the bosses I played under. Freddie Cox was very motivational, taking training sessions in shorts regardless of the weather, and sometimes joining in the end-of-training game. Basil Hayward, on the other hand, who took over from Freddie at Gillingham, very seldom took the training sessions, leaving it to the trainer. Hayward, although much younger than Cox, just stood and watched the sessions. He wasn't a great motivator, and he and I didn't get on. He actually said to me at one point that he didn't think I deserved the player of the year award that I had been given, and dropped me for the last game of the season. Not exactly the best motivation! Following Freddie to Bournemouth was an appealing prospect, as I liked his style of management, and we actually got on well. However, when he was fired and John Bond came to the club, things were very different. I understood the logic behind John's approach to the game, which paid off on the pitch – we just didn't get on that well.

During my time as a footballer, I played with and

against some very talented players. I know I could have played at a higher level if I had been more committed, but I was happy to play in the shadows of the greats. I was lucky enough to play against the likes of George Best, Emlyn Hughes, Ian St John and many more.

Most people, if they're honest, would like to leave a legacy; some lasting influence that is the sum of all the outcomes from our behaviour that others continue to remember us by. As a retired professional footballer, I would like to be remembered as a fan's favourite, and to have been liked and trusted by my fellow players. I would always give one hundred per cent to the team, whoever we were playing. I cannot remember a single professional match when I did not give my all – it was simply not in me to not give my all, whether it was Workington, Bradford, Leeds, Shaftesbury or Blandford. This attitude was taken into my next career after football, and it saw me continue to achieve things at a high level for over 40 years. Neither of my parents were very competitive, but both had a good work and life ethic, and I am sure that this is where mine comes from.

Anyway, that's it from me. I hope you enjoyed reading this book as much as I did walking back through memory lane to pull it all together!

DAVID STOCKS' BEST XIS

Throughout my career, I was fortunate enough to play with a number of great players, as well as to pit myself against some of the game's true greats. While most of them have been mentioned throughout the course of this book, I thought I'd put together two separate teams here, comprising those I played with, and those I played against. One thing's for sure: it would be one hell of a game. I've even given myself a place on the bench…

Teammates XI
Manager
John Bond, Bournemouth – A brilliant coach and tactician, but lacked people skills! He improved me as a player in the relatively short time I played for him, but as a personality I found him difficult to communicate with.

Goalkeeper
Roger Jones, Bournemouth – A great all-round goalkeeper,

a good shot stopper and a commanding presence in the box, as reflected in his England U23 call up in 1970 and subsequent transfer to Blackburn Rovers in the same year.

Defence

Terry Gulliver, Bournemouth – In my opinion, if Gully was playing today he would have been a Premier League player. He was quick, a good tackler and had excellent distribution. I would have him in my team, if only because he always seemed to attract the girls when we would venture out to the nightclubs!

Derek Harrison, Torquay – A commanding presence, excellent in the air and a good all-round defender. He arrived from Leicester in 1974 for a five-figure fee, but unfortunately suffered from injuries that curtailed his career at Torquay. He could and should have played at a higher level.

Marvin Hinton, Charlton – An absolute class act, as reflected in his England U23 appearances. Calmness personified when in possession of the ball, and an excellent reader of the game when it came to defending.

Brian Kinsey, Charlton – A solid and energetic full-back who liked to get forward to support the front players. He was originally a left winger, hence the attacking instincts. Having him in the team does mean I am relegated to the bench, unfortunately – as was often the case in real life!

Midfield

Mike Bailey, Charlton – 'Skipper' always gave one hundred per cent, hence being prone to the occasional injury. He produced the odd goal, with his biting tackles and great leadership helping him win several England caps. He would be an automatic first choice in my team.

Roy Matthews, Charlton – A classy ball-playing midfielder and an excellent passer of the ball. He chipped in with a few goals too, and was always happy to make the odd tackle to help out defensively.

Forwards

Ted MacDougall, Bournemouth – What can you say? I can't leave this goal machine out of my team. His record speaks for itself, but just in case you need reminding, he scored a club-record 49 goals in the 1970/71 season in the Third Division (including six penalties), plus seven in the FA Cup. His overall record before he left for Manchester United in September 1972 was an impressive 126 goals in 165 appearances. Saying that, he was helped greatly by his strike partner, Phil Boyer, who scored a total of 195 goals while serving with York City, Bournemouth, Norwich City and Southampton. When they were playing together in the same XI, Super Mac netted 127 and Boyer contributed 68.

Keith Peacock, Charlton – 'Snatch', as he was known, was a great goalscorer from midfield and a hard-working technician. A loyal one-club man and one of my best mates at Charlton, he made an incredible 591 appearances in all competitions – the second most in the history of the club – scoring 107 goals in the process.

Lenny Glover, Charlton – I'd have Lenny on the left wing because he was pacey and direct and got his share of goals. Another close friend at the club, we were both South London boys, and often travelled to the ground together for training and matches. He was sold to Leicester City for £80,000 during the 1967/68 season, much to the displeasure of supporters, who thought he was worth more.

Ray Bumstead, Bournemouth – A hard-working winger and consistent team player who would frequently set up opportunities for other players. A long-serving player, from May 1958 to June 1970 he scored 55 goals, and made a then-record 415 league appearances for the Cherries.

Substitutes
Eddie Firmani, Charlton – Another class act, a superb front man with an excellent goalscoring record. His game was polished by his spell in Italian football with Genoa, Sampdoria and Internazionale, and he was always happy to help other players with their game. A real gentleman.

Phil Boyer, Bournemouth – Part of the legendary MacDougall/Boyer partnership, he was a great target man with excellent ability.

David Stocks – It goes without saying that I am on the bench, as I would struggle to get in this team! Known as the 'elegant full-back' by my teammates, I had my uses on and off the pitch, especially when it involved the bar!

Opposition XI
Goalkeeper

Peter Bonetti, Chelsea – I played against him for Charlton in the FA Cup. A very athletic shot-stopper with good distribution for a goalkeeper, plus a consistent performer at the highest level over many seasons.

Defence

Bobby Moore, West Ham – My captain and defensive linchpin is none other than Mr West Ham himself. A magnificent defender and passer of the ball, his first touch was outstanding and he was always great at creating time for himself. He wasn't the quickest of defenders, but his reading of the game was brilliant; probably the best I've ever seen. He never hurried, and was always in control of the situation on the field. I played against him and Geoff Hurst when I was at Charlton in an FA Cup tie at Upton Park on 4th January 1964. I was actually playing at right-back in that match – with Kinsey on the left, I had to train all week for this change of position.

Emlyn Hughes, Liverpool – Alongside Moore at centre-back is the all-action former Liverpool captain. He would be the legs for Moore, covering any gaps left in defence and generally motivating the team.

George Cohen, Fulham – The second World Cup winner in

the back four, who I played against once while at Charlton. In my early teens, I used to go and watch Fulham play in the old First Division. Cohen was one of the best defenders I ever saw – I never once saw a winger go past him. He was very quick across the ground, a great tackler and a real old-fashioned defender, but very constructive when going forward.

Eddie McCreadie, Chelsea – He would slot in at left-back, which means I wouldn't make this team. Not that I would be next in line – Ray Wilson would probably get in ahead of me, too.

Midfield
Terry Venables, Chelsea – Probably the best all-round midfielder I played against. He had a way of controlling the game with his ability at club and international level.

John Hollins, Chelsea – To complement Venables, I have chosen John. These two together were perfect for each other: Hollins was a hard-running midfielder and tackler, and they were very successful as a pair at Chelsea.

Forwards
Ian Callaghan, Liverpool – An old-school, out-and-out right winger. When I made my debut at left-back for Charlton at Anfield, he was my primary opponent. A great provider of crosses from the wing, and chipped in with the odd goal too.

Peter Thompson, Liverpool – A fast and tricky left winger who also weighed in with a few goals. Formerly of Preston, he was a brilliant ball player, with a frightening burst of speed and accurate shooting.

Geoff Hurst, West Ham – A great goalscorer, it seemed impossible to win the ball from him when it was played up to his feet. He was the perfect all-round centre forward, as reflected in his World Cup success with England in 1966.

Jimmy Greaves, Chelsea – A goal machine both at club level and for England alongside Hurst. I played against him at schoolboy level when he was at Chelsea, but even then it was clear how good he would become.

Substitutes
George Best – On the bench here, as he wasn't at his best when I played him, but how can you not include him? Mind you, I'm not sure I would actually want to play against him again even when he was nowhere near his top form. Having met him on the pitch in a charity match at Bournemouth Poppies, he casually informed me that he was going to nutmeg me, which he promptly did – twice, much to the amusement of my teammates.

Ian St John, Liverpool – Not only a goalscorer, but also great at creating chances for other players. The perfect substitute.

Roger Hunt, Liverpool – Another out-and-out goalscorer, like St John he would be great to be thrown on when chasing the game or seeing the team over the line by keeping the ball in possession.

BIBLIOGRAPHY

Cherries: First Hundred Years - AFC Bournemouth 1899-1999, Kevin Nash (1999, Red Post Books)

The Definitive AFC Bournemouth, Leigh Edwards and John Treleven (2003, Tony Brown)

MacDou-Goal! The Ted MacDougall Story, Neil Vacher and Ted MacDougall (2006, Pitch Publishing)

Goal Along With the Cherries: The Story of Bournemouth & Boscombe Athletic's 1970/71 Promotion Season, Neil Vacher (2021, AFC Bournemouth)

No Substitute, Rick Everitt and Keith Peacock (2001, Charlton Athletic Football Club)

Football With The Millionaires, Eddie Firmani (1959, Stanley Paul)

Home & Away With Charlton Athletic, 1920-2004, Colin Cameron and Rick Everitt (2003, Voice of the Valley)

Torquay United: The Official Centenary History, 1899-1999, Leigh Edwards, Jon Gibbes and John Lovis (1999, Yore Publications)

http://gillinghamfcscrapbook.co.uk

About the authors

David Stocks was born on 20 April 1943 in London, right in the middle of the Second World War. His parents' home was demolished by a German bomb launched by the Luftwaffe – fortunately the were not in it at the time! Following a 13-year career as a professional footballer, he worked in the world of finance until retiring at the age of 75. This is his first and probably only attempt at writing a book, but he has enjoyed the trip down memory lane and hopes you do too!

Stephen Wright grew up next door to David in Wimborne, Dorset. He made up for his lack of footballing ability by obsessing about it in every other way, and jumped at the chance to help David write his autobiography. He has been an AFC Bournemouth season ticket holder from a young age, and works in publishing as an editor, writer and sub editor. Titles he has worked on include SciFiNow, How It Works, Digital Camera and All About History. He can be contacted at stevewright273@gmail.com.